Dear
G.I.R.L.S.

Thya

 Simeaka Melton

Published by Simeaka Melton

Copyright © 2015 written by Simeaka Melton

ISBN: 150557644X
ISBN-13 9781505576443

ACKNOWLEDGMENTS

I Thank God For Choosing Me **Jeremiah 29:11**

My Grandmothers
Lillian Curtis, Sylvia Johnson, Anna Taylor and Henrietta Hynson

Mother
Linda Faye Taylor

My Mommy
Sheila Elias

My Mom
Fatima Johnson

My Fairy God Mother
Arlene Taylor

My Mother In Law
Frankie Melton

My Aunties, My Sisters, My Nieces

My Daughter
Little Miss Aaliyah. My gift, my reason for my creations and my why to preserve.

For Every Girl
who has gifted me the privilege to love, serve, empower, teach and impact through my purpose.

For Every Girl In The World

The Mothers and Women Of The Church Who I Watched Watching Me

The Women In The Village

"Thank You" to my fathers
Larry Taylor Sr. AND Howard Johnson Jr.

It's On All Their Shoulders I Stand.

DEDICATIONS

This book is dedicated to Aaliyah, Christian, Jevon, Deonte and Jshuane, the gifted elements of my life.

DEDICATIONS

To my beautiful daughter.

Dear Aaliyah,

I love you with all my heart. You are truly a gift from the Lord. I am blessed with the gifted of being your mother and to witness you grow up into a special young lady. I am truly very proud of you already. You are the why to the creation of this book. My prayer for you is that you continue to demonstrate your natural instincts: love, truth and kindness. Build upon all the qualities written in this book and beyond. Make your imprint on the world with integrity, purpose, perseverance and love, unapologetically.

.

DEDICATIONS

To my brilliant sons.

Dear Christian, Jevon and Deonte,

You have already shown signs of becoming great men and I could not be prouder. This book is also for you. The lessons in this book are timeless and are lessons you can build upon. When the time comes and you choose wives and if you are blessed with daughters remember these lessons to teach them. As for today, individually you are the light that allows me to see *beyond* beyond. My prayer for you is that you unapologetically become the change you want to see in this world and do it all with integrity, purpose, perseverance and love. Always live as men of honor.

DEDICATIONS

To my amazing husband.

Dear Jshuane,

You are my everything. Because of you loving me in the most amazing ways, wrapping your arms around my gifts, unconditionally being my purpose pusher, my very best friend, my rock, my provider, my protector, my laughter, my light and being my biggest support and the voice of truth and reason "we" were able to make this book possible. The word does not exist that explains how much you mean to me so I will simply say I love you AND thank you. I love you with all my heart and a whole lot more. My prayer for you is that you continue to shock the world with your gifts and that all the desires of your heart be granted ten fold. I love you beyond the moon and back.

Dear Girls

Activate Your Girl Power!

The Ultimate Girls
Go-To Guide
For Activating GIRL POWER

TABLE OF CONTENTS

TABLE OF CONTENTS

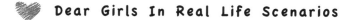 **Dear Girls In Real Life Scenarios**

TABLE OF CONTENTS

TABLE OF CONTENTS

"When life gives you a puzzle you just have to activate your girl power and solve it!"

Aaliyah Melton

Lesson #1

Girl Power

"There is no power like girl power. Never ever give it away."

Simeaka Melton

Dear Girls,

Guess what? You have Girl Power! You are more powerful than you even realize!

Your girl power is in the freedom of being a girl. You can make your own decisions about what you like, what your interests are. You can enjoy the things you like without feeling guilty, be proud of the things you do well, create and achieve big dreams, and have lots of fun! That's girl power!

You can become whatever you decide. All because you have girl power! There is something very special about being a girl.

When you shrink who you are and who you were created to be to please others, you give your power away.

15

There is no power like Girl Power! Never ever give it away!

Activate Your Girl Power!

Lesson #1

Girl Power

Girl Power! Activate! Go! Do you feel it? One of the greatest things about being a girl is having girl power! Yes, Girl Power! Activate! Go!

Naturally, you possess Girl Power. You may have to discover it but you absolutely have it, all girls have it! You were born with it.

Your Girl Power is your self-love, your self-confidence and is in your freedom to be your unique self. You are smart, daring, beautiful, loved, bold, kind, gifted, important, priceless and intentional.

You have the freedom to make your own decisions about what you like, what your interests are, enjoy the things you like without feeling guilty, be proud of the things you do well, create and achieve big dreams, and having lots of fun! Girl Power is the special part about being a girl.

Have you ever had a friend that was good at something but didn't want to do it because she was worried about what others would say about her? Or have you ever decided not to do something because you didn't want others to judge or make fun of you? Or how about this one, have you or a friend ever liked a boy and decided not to do something or do well at something because of what the boy might think about you? Well, those are all examples of giving your Girl Power away.

There is no power like Girl Power so never ever give it way. Your girl power belongs to you so enjoy it. It isn't something someone can give you; you were born with it; no one can take it from you. The only way you lose it is to give it away so protect it.

Protect your Girl Power by doing things that empower you, things that get you closer to your dreams, not letting anyone trick you into believing you are not good enough, and by believing in yourself enough to work hard at your dreams and goals.

Girl Power! Activate! Go! Do you feel it now? If you don't you will and when you own your Girl Power your life will be positively changed!

What is Girl Power?

A. The freedom to be your unique self
B. The chance to play dress up with friends
C. Hoping your dreams come true

When should you give your Girl Power away?

A. Always
B. Sometimes
C. Never

The only way you loose your Girl Power is to give it away.　　**TRUE** or **FALSE**

Explain a time when you had to use your Girl Power.

_____

_____

_____

_____

_____

_____

_____

_____

Dear Diary #1

Meet Adele. Adele loves to draw and has been thinking about entering a drawing contest. Adele wrote about it in her diary.

June 24th

Dear Diary,

Today my best friend, Janae, reminded me that the deadline to enter the state drawing contest is Friday! She thinks my drawings are great!

I told Morris that I was thinking of entering the contest and he laughed. Morris is this boy that I like. He draws really well too so I thought we could enter the contest together for fun but he didn't think so.

Morris said he didn't like my drawings because they were weird. Maybe I need to practice some more and wait until next year to enter the contest.

Actually maybe I shouldn't show Morris my drawings until I get a little better.

Or maybe I should stop drawing for a while and do something else. Well there is always next year right?

Well if I even keep drawing, that is.

Love,

Adele

Simeaka Melton

Lesson #1 Journal Entry

What do you think about Adele not entering the drawing contest? Write a letter to let her letting her know what you think about her decision.

Date _____

Dear Adele,

_____
_____
_____
_____
_____
_____
_____
_____
_____
_____
_____
_____
_____
_____
_____
_____
_____
_____
_____
_____

Love,

_____

Lesson #2

You Are Enough

"You are not only good enough you are great enough."

Simeaka Melton

Dear Girls,

You are enough. You are not only good enough you are great enough. Do not ever let anyone trick you into believing anything different. Do not try to change who you are to fit in with your friends or anyone else. Work hard, be kind, have fun and never give up because you are enough. You are great enough to do whatever you believe enough to work hard at doing!

Lesson #2

You Are Enough

Has anyone ever told you that you are enough? As you are at this very moment, you are enough. You are smart enough, pretty enough, fun enough, important enough. You are enough.

You are enough means that you do not have to do anything extra to be "as good as" someone else. You are enough means you are automatically equal to others.

You were born enough.

Since the beginning of time, girls everywhere, at one time or another have thought they were not good enough or have felt as though they did not measure up in some way. The reason girls feel this way is because someone else has made them feel insecure about something about themselves.

Girls are often tricked into believing that they are not enough because of other people's insecurities.

Enjoy and be comfortable with who you are. You have nothing to prove because you are enough just the way you are. Do not waste any time wishing you were something that you already are because you are already enough.

You are not only good enough you are great enough.

What does being enough mean?

A. You are a good friend.
B. Everyone likes you.
C. You are automatically as equal as others.

I feel less confident around other girls who can do something better than me.

A. Always
B. Sometimes
C. Never

You do not need to prove to anyone that you are good enough.   **TRUE** or **FALSE**

Write four positive statements about yourself.

1._____

2._____

3._____

4._____

Dear Diary #2

Meet Angela. Her friend Barbara had a sleepover and Angela was not invited. Angela wrote about it in her diary.

September 29th

Dear Diary,

Today at school I overheard Lisa and Marie talking about how much fun they had at Barbara's sleepover this past weekend! I didn't know anything about it. If Barbara is my friend why wasn't I invited? Lisa and Marie are both on the dance team and are both pretty. That's probably why I wasn't invited. I'm not good at anything but basketball. And I certainly can not dance. Maybe I will stop being friends with Barbara for while or at least until I learn how to dance or do something like the other girls. Well gotta go!

Love,

Angela

Dear Girls In Real Life Scenarios

Lesson #2 Journal Entry

Angela seems to be feeling left out. Write a letter to Angela about how she is feeling.

Date _____

Dear Angela,

_____
_____
_____
_____
_____
_____
_____
_____
_____
_____
_____
_____
_____
_____
_____
_____
_____
_____
_____
_____

Love,

_____

Lesson #3

Friends Are
The Best

"The company you keep matters at every age."

Simeaka Melton

Dear Girls,

Choose your friends carefully. Be a good friend to people who are good friends to you. You will meet people who are fun to be around but may not be a good friend to you. When people don't make good friends, it's okay to be nice to them but that does not mean you have to friends; just be friendly.

Make sure that when you have good friends, you treat them equally as nice because that helps build a good and long lasting friendship.

The company you keep matters so choose your friends carefully.

Lesson #3

Friends Are The Best

The company you keep matters at every age. Who you choose as friends often shows how you feel about yourself. If you choose to be friends with people who treat you badly or say mean things to you, it may be because you feel unloved or unworthy or you may feel like you may not be able to get any other friends. You deserve friends that respect you and treat you well. It shows that your respect and value yourself.

You will meet lots of people who will make good friends, so be kind to people who treat you nice, say nice things to you and to tell you good things when you feel bad about something or about yourself because that just might be a good friend.

Your friends should also make good decisions and have values that are aligned with yours. The old saying "birds of a feather flock together" proves to be true in time.

Some important things to remember when you are choosing friends:

1. Friends do not intentionally make you feel bad about yourself.

2. Friends do not make fun of you.

3. Friends do not ignore your feelings.

4. Friends make you laugh.

5. Friends encourage you to do your best.

6. Friends are nice, they believe in you, respect you, help you and love you.

Friends are the best! You do not have try to do things to make people like you other than be the type of friend you want others to be to you.

What makes a good friend?

A. Living in the same neighborhood.
B. Encouraging one another to do their best.
C. Treating one another nice sometimes.

Friends should respect your feelings

A. Always
B. Sometimes
C. Never

Good friends make fun of you so no one else does. TRUE or FALSE

What do most value about your friends?

_____
_____
_____
_____
_____
_____
_____
_____
_____
_____
_____

Dear Diary #3

Meet Danielle. Danielle and Rebecca are very best friends. They both like to fashion, nail polish and pink! Danielle wrote about it in her diary.

Dear Diary,

Guess what! Danielle and I were both chosen by our teacher to be in charge of the fashion show. I am so excited I can hardly wait! Score!

Here's the thing, today at lunch Rebecca and I were telling the other girls about it and Rebecca really hurt my feelings. In front of everyone Rebecca turned to me and said "I don't know why you were chosen because you know nothing about fashion." and all the girls began to laugh.

It was so embarrassing I could have cried but that would have even worse.

Later I asked Rebecca why did she say that because it hurt my

Lesson #4

Refuse Defeat

"Fight like a girl and refuse defeat."
Simeaka Melton

Dear Girls,

Refuse defeat! We do not always accomplish every goal that we have but if you keep trying you will not be defeated.

When you get disappointed by not achieving your goals, do not ever give up on yourself. Do not become defeated by disappointing results. Fight like a girl to achieve your goals. Keep trying until you reach your goals.

Refuse defeat!

Lesson #4

Refuse Defeat

In life ,we all experience disappointments. Sometimes disappointments will make your feel defeated. Defeat is when you have quit. Not every goal you have will turn out the way you plan but the way you respond to your disappointments determines how well you are able to bounce back.

You refuse defeat when you do not give

up and quit. Not achieving your goals can be disappointing but when that happens if you have done your best it's okay.

There is nothing to be embarrassed of or ashamed about. Try again, try another way or simply try something new but never give up on yourself. If you keep trying you will not be defeated. That's how you refuse defeat, by trying again and again.

There will be things you do well and things you do not do so well and that's perfectly okay. There will be things you achieve and things you do not achieve. That is also okay. In fact no one can do everything extremely well. Find the things you enjoy doing well and continue doing them. Try new things often because you never know how good you can be at something if you do not discover it for yourself. Refuse defeat!

How do you refuse defeat?

A. Give up after you are disappointed.
B. Keep trying new things.
C. Get someone else to try for you.

When should you give up on yourself?

A. Always
B. Sometimes
C. Never

If you get embarrassed my disappointing results its okay to give up.

TRUE or **FALSE**

What will you do if you do not get the results you want if your goal is not accomplished? Explain why.

_____
_____
_____
_____
_____
_____
_____
_____

Dear Diary #4

Meet Sylvia. Sylvia loves to bake. Her family loves when she bakes for them. She has decided to sell her cupcakes at the school bake sale. Sylvia wrote about it in her diary.

September 23rd

Dear Diary,

Guess what!!! I decided to bake my delicious cupcakes and sell them at our school bake sale! BUT today at school I asked my friends to buy my cupcakes that I made and only one person brought one measly cupcake.

To make matters worse, one boy even said my chocolate cupcakes look like poop! I was so mad and so embarrassed. I will never try to sell those cupcakes ever again. Maybe my cupcakes aren't that good or maybe they do look like poop. I don't know but I don't think I will be baking any time soon. I feel so defeated because I only sold one cupcake and everyone else sold a lot of everything. I give up!

That's it for me! I'm done with baking!

Love,

Sylvia

Lesson #4 Journal Entry

With just one cupcake sold, Sylvia wants to give up. Write Sylvia letter about her dilemma.

Date _____

Dear Sylvia,

_____
_____
_____
_____
_____
_____
_____
_____
_____
_____
_____
_____
_____
_____
_____
_____
_____
_____
_____
_____
_____
_____

Love,

_____

48

Lesson #5

Be A Smart Girl

"After the dream, write your vision to accomplish great things."

Simeaka Melton

Dear Girls,

Smart girls have goals. S.M.A.R.T. Goals. Dreaming big is the beginning and setting goals is key. Your goals should be Specific, Measurable, Attainable, Realistic and have Timelines. A dream without S.M.A.R.T. goals will remain a dream. Be S.M.A.R.T.

Lesson #5

Be A
S.M.A.R.T. Girl

S.M.A.R.T. Girls rock the world! In order to be a S.M.A.R.T. girl you must have S.M.A.R.T. goals. Your goals should be specific, measurable, attainable, realistic, and have timelines. To achieve great things your planning matters and you should plan smart. Write down your

51

goals, study ways to get you closer to your goals, work towards your goals and don't let anyone talk you out of your goal.

Plan, prepare and proceed.

Be a S.M.A.R.T. girl!

S.M.A.R.T.

Specific - Your goal should be **clear**.

Measurable - Your goal should explain **how** you will accomplish your goal.

Attainable - Your goal should be something **sensible.**

Realistic - Your goal should be something **real** and something that can happen.

Timelines - Your goal should have **dates** about the details of how you plan to accomplish your goal.

Dear Girls In Real Life Scenarios

Quiz #5

List four of your goals below.

_____

_____

_____

_____

Name one of the goals that you would like to make
S.M.A.R.T.

_____

_____

What do you want to accomplish? MAKE IT
<u>SPECIFIC</u>. (clear)

_____

_____

_____

_____

How will you know when you have accomplished
your goal? MAKE IT <u>MEASURABLE</u>. (how)

_____

_____

_____

_____

How can your goal be accomplished? MAKE IT
ATTAINABLE. (sensible)

_____
_____
_____
_____

Is this goal worth working hard to accomplish?

_____

Explain your reason. MAKE IT REALISTIC.
(real)

_____
_____
_____
_____

When will your goal be accomplished? MAKE
TIMELINES. (dates)

_____
_____
_____
_____
_____

How will you know when you have accomplished your goal? MAKE IT <u>MEASURABLE.</u>   (how)

_____

_____

_____

_____

_____

_____

_____

_____

Simeaka Melton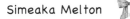

Lesson #5 Journal Entry
Write about how you feel about being a smart girl.

Date _____

Dear Diary,

_____
_____
_____
_____
_____
_____
_____
_____
_____
_____
_____
_____
_____
_____
_____
_____
_____
_____
_____
_____
_____

Love,

_____

Lesson #6

Fearfully and Wonderfully Made

"The things that make you different also make you special."

Simeaka Melton

Dear Girls,

The world is sending you tons of bogus messages of what to believe about yourself. Messages like: You are less than, You need to have more, You need to be more, You are not enough, You are not pretty enough, You are not thin enough, You do not measure up, are all bogus message from society. The messages are limitless and the lies are countless.

The truth is that you are fearfully and wonderfully made just as you are. Everything about you is intentional. Embrace the things that make you different, unique, stand out or even feel awkward from time to time.

You are awesome. You are smart. You are beautiful. You are loved.

You are talented. You have things about you that make you different than other girls and that is makes you pretty special.

Appreciate all those things because they are intentional gifts. There is no one else exactly like you because you are born to be different. Enjoy it because you are fearfully and wonderfully made!

Lesson #6

Fearfully and Wonderfully Made

Get excited! You are fearfully and wonderfully made! Celebrate who you are! We were all born to be different and special in our own unique ways. Even if you are a twin, there are things about you that make you distinctive. So do not confuse being different with being wrong. Being different is not a disadvantage; it's a gift. Enjoy everything about you that makes you who you are.

Girls have many differences and sometimes, we see our difference as a bad thing. Not so. Your difference could be a gap in your teeth, freckles on your face, your height, your hair, a limp in your walk, a squeaky voice, a big nose, darker skin or lighter skin BUT regardless of the difference, you are fearfully and wonderfully made with love.

Do not compare yourself to other girls, or images seen on television, in magazines, across billboards or even in your classroom. You can never be someone or something you were born not to be. You were born to be different. You were born to be yourself. Have fun being yourself!

Quiz #6

The things that make you different are

A. a mistake and weird
B. a shame and funny
C. intentional and special

You should celebrate your differences and who you are

A. Always
B. Sometimes
C. Never

You were born fearfully and wonderfully made.   **TRUE** or **FALSE**

Name four things that make you fearfully and wonderfully made.

1._____
2._____
3._____
4._____

Meet Gina! Gina and her friend Jen have new friends and Jen is having a sleepover! Gina wrote about it in her diary.

February 16th

Dear Diary,

Yesterday Jen and I hung out with a few girls from our math class. We looked at magazines, did our nails, we talked about boys, took a few pictures and danced. It was fun for the most part but I feel weird being around them because they're all so cool! Like really cool. They're all so pretty, they dress really cool, they know everything, everyone likes them, and they are really popular. I bet they all could be models or something.

OMG! Jen said on Saturday she's going to have a sleepover! She made a point to tell me to ask mom if I could ride the bus home with her on Friday. Yikes! It's not that I don't want to go I just don't feel like I fit in because those girls are perfect.

I'm the only one with freckles, I'm the only one with glasses, plus I'm a lot shorter. I hate to even think about how I will look in pictures with them. No thank you!

Love,

Gina

Lesson #6 Journal Entry

Gina is feeling really insecure. Write Gina letter about her how she feels.

Date _____

Dear Gina,

_____
_____
_____
_____
_____
_____
_____
_____
_____
_____
_____
_____
_____
_____
_____
_____
_____
_____
_____
_____
_____

Love,

_____

Lesson #7

Inner Image

"Your inner image reveals your true beauty."

Simeaka Melton

Dear Girls,

Your inner image reflects your true beauty. Beauty comes from the inside and shines through to the outside. Our true character is merely the evidence of our inner beauty. Don't be fooled by the type of beauty that reflects in the mirror.

Our heart is the most beautiful part of ourselves. Make up does not make you beautiful; it only enhances your features. It does not create your beauty. Real beauty comes from within.

Your inner image is seen by the things you do naturally. The way you speak, treat others, make decisions and all the things you do when no one is watching.

Your inner image is beauty that last forever.

Lesson #7

Inner Image

Your inner image tells the story of who you truly are. Your inner image is the characteristic of your personality. Society has dismissed the value of inner image and in turn encourages us to focus on outer beauty. Their countless messages imply our outer beauty is most important. Society also presents distorted images to be claimed as real beauty.

Lies, lies and more lies. The truth is your inner beauty is what lasts, matters and is what shows up regardless of make up.

Your inner beauty is shown through your inner image. The beauty of your inner image is the beauty that never fades. Your inner image is your true character. It's the love you show others, the acts of kindness you give to your family, friends and even strangers. Your inner image is also the attitude you display when things are going your way and when they are not going your way; it's your natural instinct without hesitation or second thoughts.

Let's discover what makes our inner image beautiful or not. Our self confidence, self love and self esteem are what makes up our inner beauty. How we feel about ourselves and how we treat others determines our true beauty.

Our inner image is connected to our souls so it should always be full of beauty.

Too often, society sends messages that girls need to change or improve their beauty. To trick girls into believing the messages from society that we are bombarded with countless billboards, magazines photos, television advertisements and plenty of photo shopped images. All screaming "Change"! "Change your hair, lips, eyes, hands, feet, legs, hips, body ... change you".

Society says every girl needs make up to be beautiful. The truth is your inner image requires no make up because it's made of all your personal and natural personality character traits. Your inner image reveals your true beauty.

What every girl needs in her "Inner Image Make Up Kit"

#1 Lips
Speak words that uplift.
Words of kindness, truth, love, encouragement, honor, respect and words that build each other up and never to break down.

#2 Eyes
Use your eyes to see the good in the world and to recognize the not so good in the world.
Nevertheless, look for the good in things and in others. There is a blessing in everything.

#3 Hands
Your hands can show love.
Use your hands to provide services to others. What better way to show love and compassion than to provide service to others and random acts of kindness.

#4 Feet

Stand on your values.

Stand for what's right even if you stand alone. Standing up for yourself and stand for things that matter. It may be hard but it will be well worth it.

#5 Legs

Stay humble and compassionate.

You never truly understand someone else's story unless you have walked a mile in their shoes.

Never judge, rather stay humble and compassionate.

#6 Hips

Dance! Celebrate!

Life is to be celebrated regardless of your circumstance. Enjoy the good things in life, share goodness with people who care and spread the love.

Dear Girls In Real Life Scenarios

Quiz #7

Your inner image is

A. the image you see in the mirror
B. the characteristics of your personality
C. your good days personality

You under value your inner image

A. Always
B. Sometimes
C. Never

Your inner image requires no make up.

TRUE or **FALSE**

Explain how important your inner image is to you.

_____
_____
_____
_____
_____
_____
_____
_____

Dear Diary #7

*Meet Skylar. Skylar is having friendship trouble. She wrote
all about them in her diary.*

November 16th

Dear Diary,

I've been friends with Denise since
we were both in the 2nd grade and
we have always had lots of fun.
Well here's the trouble. We got a
new girl in our class named Molly
and every since she came, Denise
has been acting different.

Actually I think Denise has turned
into a MEAN GIRL, just like Molly. I
do not like to be negative, or mean
or rude but these two are
unbelievable. They talk down to
people, they talk about people, they
act like they are better than
everybody and they compare
themselves celebrities and super
stars all the time.

To make matters worse my birthday
is coming up and I do not want

them to come. I mean I would like
them to come but I don't want to
around mean girls. They don't treat
me mean but it's awkward being
around them sometimes.

Yesterday our friend Kayla spilled
her milk at breakfast, and Denise
did nothing to help and Molly
laughed. When I helped her they
both made me feel bad about
helping.

I thought about just having Kayla
come over because she's a good
friend, and I like her a lot but I
don't know what to do about Denise
and Molly. I'm so confused.

TTYL xoxoxoxoxoxoxo :)

Love,

Skylar

Lesson #7 Journal Entry

Skylar is feeling confused. Write Skylar letter about her how she feels.

Date _____

Dear Skylar,

_____
_____
_____
_____
_____
_____
_____
_____
_____
_____
_____
_____
_____
_____
_____
_____
_____
_____
_____
_____

Love,

_____

Lesson #8

Dreams, Goals and Boys

"Smart girls follow their dreams not boys."

Simeaka Melton

Dear Girls,

Follow your dreams and goals not boys! You have plenty of time for boys! Boys are not going anywhere but your dreams may if you lose focus. One of the most valuable relationships that you will ever have will be the relationship that you have with yourself. You are enough and you are worthy.

When you decide to have a relationship with a boy, be sure that he honors you, respects you, values you and treats you well.

When love becomes a factor, you must first love yourself. Do not settle for less just to have someone. Do not ever settle for someone that tolerates you, he must appreciate you. You are worth more than you think and you are worthy of love, respect and friendship.

Dream big! Have goals! Write them down!

Use your imagination! Using your imagination simply means to see yourself doing something before you actually do it. Dream BIG, write down your plans and accomplish great things.

Do not get distracted by boys ... no matter how cute they might appear to be!

Lesson #8

Dreams, Goals and Boys

Your mind is one of your greatest assets. Dream big, set high goals, write them down, work hard and you will accomplish great things in this world.

Don't just have any ordinary dream or a typical goal, make your dreams big and have grand and golden goals. Be sure to use your imagination to discover all your gifts and talents. Spend time doing things you like and love. Don't be scared to try new things because you never know what you can do until discover the things you do well for yourself.

Never "dumb down" your greatness. Do not change who you are, to be liked or to be considered or to fit in with the friends.

As you grow up, experience new things and encounter new people. There will be lots of distractions. The key is staying focused on your dreams and goals.

When you find a boy you like, choose him carefully. He should be more than cute. He must respect and value you and treat you well. It is important to stay focused and to not let boys become a distraction.

Follow your dreams and goals not boys! It

is easy for boys to become a distraction because it's something new, fun and interesting.

From time to time friends will try to convince you to do what's fun instead of what's necessary. Sometimes doing what's necessary, like homework, chores, following the rules, or even practicing an instrument or sports, might not be as fun but it will definitely be worth it.

Doing what's necessary develops your character and determines how, when and if you will accomplish your goals. When we do the things that we have to do, we give ourselves so many opportunities and choices to do what we want to do and that is *very* fun!

If you believe you can do it and if you are willing to commit to working very hard you can achieve your goals.

Dream big, set goals

A. write, draw and follow the crowd
B. write them down and work hard
C. write a song and work hard

"Dumb down" your greatness

A. Always
B. Sometimes
C. Never

Boys should respect and value you.

TRUE or **FALSE**

What does dumb down mean?

_____
_____
_____
_____
_____
_____
_____
_____
_____
_____

Dear Diary #8

Meet Laniyah! Laniyah is a great science student and likes a boy in her class. You won't believe what happened. Laniyah wrote about it in her diary.

August 23rd

Dear Diary,

Andrew is the cutest boy in my class and he likes me. Connie told me that he talks about me all the time. Our teacher paired the students with high grades with the students with lower grades. Guess who my partner is? Yes Andrew! Andrew gets D's in science and I get A's and B's. So Ms. Hyson wants us to work together.

Here's the problem. I can't help Andrew because he will feel bad that I have better grades than him and he might not like me. Ms. Hyson said if I do a good job she will let me help her during summer school because she knows I want to be a science teacher when I grow up but what about Andrew. If he thinks I am smarter than him, he might not like me anymore. I got it! I will tell Ms. Hyson that I can't help Andrew because I have something important to do and she should get someone else. Maybe I can help her next year because Andrew is way too cute to worry about science right now.

Love,

Laniyah

Simeaka Melton

Lesson #8 Journal Entry

What do you think about Laniyah's decision? Write Laniyah a letter before she makes a mistake.

Date _____

Dear Laniyah,

_____
_____
_____
_____
_____
_____
_____
_____
_____
_____
_____
_____
_____
_____
_____
_____
_____
_____
_____
_____
_____
_____
_____

Love,

_____

Lesson #9

I D.A.R.E. You

"I dare you to live life rising above expectations."

Simeaka Melton

Dear Girls,

I D.A.R.E. you to be your BEST self.

I D.A.R.E. you to comfort with your differences.

I D.A.R.E. you to think outside of the box.

I D.A.R.E. you to love yourself despite what others think or says.

I D.A.R.E. you to be the change you want to see.

I D.A.R.E. you because you are powerful enough to accomplish whatever you D.A.R.E. to work hard for.

D.A.R.E. to be treat yourself great!

I D.A.R.E. you to shock the world.

I D.A.R.E. you to use your imagination.

I D.A.R.E. you to create the life that you desire.

I D.A.R.E. you to live life rising above expectations!

Lesson #9

I D.A.R.E. You

Sometimes, we do not have the courage to be ourselves because we don't what to be judged by others or may feel embarrassed to stand out amongst of friends.

What others think of you should not concern you. Just be yourself. In everything you do, dare to be your best self.

The Webster's Dictionary definition of the word **DARE** is_ *to have enough courage or confidence to do something.*

Do you have enough courage or confidence to do something that others think you should not do? Do you have enough courage or confidence to do something that you may think is too hard for you to do? Do you have enough courage or confidence to do something new? Do you have enough courage or confidence to stand out?

It's natural to wonder how to (*dare*) have courage or confidence to do something.

Listed below are tips how you can dare to have enough courage or confidence to do something.

D.A.R.E.

1. D.A.R.E.

Decide you are worth your own greatness

and be **Determined** to accomplish your goals.

2. D.**A**.R.E.

Assert yourself in the world that wants to silence your input.
Aspire to greatness.

3. D.A.**R**.E.

Rise. Live your life rising above expectations. **Regardless** of circumstances.

4. D.A.R.**E.**

Embrace your differences.
Be **empower** to inspire others.

I **D.A.R.E. You** to be your best self!

I **D.A.R.E. You** to live life rising above expectations!

You can do it! Go! Have fun!

Quiz #9

DARE means

A. Not to do something you are afraid of because it hard
B. To know what to do but not do it
C. To have the enough courage and confidence to do something

If you think others will judge you for trying something new you should do it anyway.

A. Always
B. Sometimes
C. Never

If you are not good at something you should not try.   **TRUE** or **FALSE**

Explain how you will dare to be your best self.

_____
_____
_____
_____
_____
_____

Dear Diary #9

Miya does not like to be the center of attention and she has just been chosen for the lead in her school play. Miya wrote about it in her diary.

October 8th

Dear Diary,

It happened! Mrs. Hardaway chose me to be sing lead in our school play! At first I got really excited but then I thought about what everyone would say about me.

They might say I think I'm special or they might make fun of me or laugh at me or I might mess up. I was going to ask Mrs. Hardaway if I could play a different role but I kinda want to do it. I love to sing when nobody is around, I just don't want anyone to make fun of me.

I don't want to disappointment Mrs. Hardaway but I don't think I am ready to sing LEAD!

Maybe if I tell Mrs. Hardaway I can't do it because my throat is really sore, she will believe me. And maybe she won't be mad. I don't know what to do. I am so nervous. I will tell Mrs. Hardaway tomorrow.

Love,

Miya

Dear Girls In Real Life Scenarios

Lesson #9 Journal Entry

What do you think about Miya's situation? Write her a letter maybe you can help.

Date _____

Dear Miya,

_____
_____
_____
_____
_____
_____
_____
_____
_____
_____
_____
_____
_____
_____
_____
_____
_____
_____
_____
_____
_____
_____

Love,

_____

Lesson #10

Because I Said So

"Because I said so is my explanation and my answer."

Simeaka Melton

Dear Girls,

Have you ever asked someone a question and they replied, **"Because I Said So."** ?

The words **"Because I Said So."** has a sense of authority. There is no negotiating, no explanation required, and it's final.

We have so many influences in life. Some positive and some negative. With the amount of negative influences in society such as the media, music, magazines, celebrity influence and peer pressure you must take a **"Because I Said So."** approach to living above any negative influences of our surroundings.

Lesson #10
Because I Said So

To survive the many negative influences in life, a **"Because I Said So."** attitude is a must! Society, the media, music, magazines, celebrity influence, reality television, our peers and peer pressures can have a big influence on how we view ourselves. You must take a **"Because I Said So."** approach to living above the daily negative influences seen everywhere.

"Because I Said So." has a sense of authority. It gives you the authority to make decisions that empower you regardless of the reactions of others. There is no negotiating, no compromising, no explanation required, it's final and there no questions asked.

Make **"Because I Said So."** an unapologetic lifestyle to protect your destiny. Stand firmly on your decisions of greatness, value and purpose. You do not need approval or validations from your peers who are likely unqualified to do so. Seek answers from adults you trust and who have your best interest in mind.

The 'Because I Said So' Life Style

A. is a way to be mean and do whatever you want

B. gives you the authority to make decisions that empower you

C. to make others do what you want them to do

Society, the media, music, magazines, celebrity influence, reality television, our peers and peer pressure have an influence on the way we view ourselves

A. Always

B. Sometimes

C. Never

You should get approval from your peers before your make a decision to do the right thing.

TRUE or FALSE

Dear Girls In Real Life Scenarios

What can you take a 'Because I Said So'
approach to?

_____

_____

_____

_____

_____

_____

_____

_____

Dear Diary #10

Hanna and Camille are best friends. They are attending to the back school dance and want something new to wear. Hanna wrote about it in her dairy.

Dear Diary,

Camille and I went to the mall today! We saw the perfect dresses to wear to the dance. Judy's mom lets her wear whatever she wants to but my mom is such a stick in the mud. All the girls are wearing dresses like the ones we saw in the mall today. We see dresses like those in the music videos. Camille said I would be a chicken if I didn't get the dress plus all the girls will ask me why I didn't get it. What would I tell them?

Uggghhh!!! I need that dress and I know if I ask my mom she will say no. Maybe I should stay at Camille's house and my mom will never know. That's not wrong because technically I didn't even ask about the dress so she can't so

no. I sure don't want to be the
only one without one of those
dresses.

I can't wait until the dance it's
gonna be so much fun!

                         Love,

                           Hanna

Lesson #10 Journal Entry

Hanna could use some advice. Write her a letter about her decision.

Date _____

Dear Hanna,

_____

_____

_____

_____

_____

_____

_____

_____

_____

_____

_____

_____

_____

_____

_____

_____

_____

_____

_____

_____

_____

_____

Love,

_____

Lesson #11

No Is A Complete Sentence

"No is a complete sentence and a right that we all have."

Simeaka Melton

Dear Girls,

"No" is a complete sentence in itself. Stand up for yourself. Say "No" to all the things that do not empower you or make a better person. It's perfectly okay to say "No" without an explanation to negative things. You have the right to say "No" to gossip, stealing, drugs, sex, cheating, lying, and to all the things you know are wrong. You have the right to say "No" without an approval from your friends.

If you begin to explain why you say "No" to things that are wrong it can create an opportunity for negotiation. Your values are non negotiable. "No" is enough. "No" is a complete sentence. "No" is a right that we all have, so you can say "No" without feeling guilty.

Lesson #11

No Is A
Complete Sentence

"No" is a complete sentence. Sometimes you can be afraid of saying no to something because you don't want to be judge or don't wan to hurt someone's feeling. When it comes to doing what's right you come first. No is a right that we all have. You have the authority to say no without an explanation. No is all the explanation required because no is a complete sentence.

Peer pressure is one of the hardest things to say no to without explanation and surely without guilt. Feeling guilty is one of the reasons some people do things that they know they shouldn't.

Give yourself permission to say no without explanation and without feeling guilty. You have the right not to be a part of negativity.

There is a long list to what you can say no to without explanation and without guilt.

1. Lying
2. Cheating
3. Stealing
4. Drugs
5. Sex
6. Smoking cigarettes
7. Breaking the rules

8. Peer pressure
9. Drinking alcohol
10. Being mean to others
11. Following the crowd
12. Doing anything you know you should not be doing

The list goes on and on and on. Surely you can find so many additional things that could also be added to this list. Understand you have the authority to say no regardless. You do not need to explain your reason for saying no when you are doing the right thing. You do not need to negotiate doing the right thing because your values, rights and choices are non negotiable.

No is a complete sentence.

Quiz #11

No is a complete

A. Compromise
B. Negotiation
C. Sentence

Friends will be angry when you say no to something they want you to do, even if that something is wrong.

A. Always
B. Sometimes
C. Never

When you are doing the right thing you should explain so you can get the approval from your friends. **TRUE** or **FALSE**

Explain a time when you had to say no and do the right thing.

_____

_____

_____

_____

_____

Dear Diary #11

Meet Grace. She has lots of friends and needs to make a decision. Grace wrote about it in her diary.

July 31st

Dear Diary,

I really like make up but my parents say I'm too young. Blah Blah Blah! All the girls in my class already wear make up. Some girls wear red lip gloss, some girls wear all colored lip stick, some girls wear a little blush and some wear that eye stuff. Some even girls wear it all. I only want to wear a little make up but my parents don't understand that these days it's okay for girls to wear make up. Actually these days you have to wear make up. It's our style. No one wants a naked face!

I bet at Cydnee's sleep over they are all going to have their lip glosses and make up kits and wanting to try it on and play around in it.

111

We're all going roller skating in the morning and I bet they will want to put on their make up. I can't just say no, maybe I can say I'm allergic? Yeah I will say I'm allergic when they ask me why. Then they wont make fun of me. Yup that should work!

Love,

Grace

Dear Girls In Real Life Scenarios

What do you think about Grace saying she is allergic? Write her a letter about what you think.

Date _____

Dear Grace,

_____

_____

_____

_____

_____

_____

_____

_____

_____

_____

_____

_____

_____

_____

_____

_____

_____

_____

_____

_____

_____

Love,

_____

Lesson #12

Speak P.I.N.K.

"Don't be a gossip girl. There is nothing P.I.N.K. about it."

Simeaka Melton

Dear Girls,

You will be surprised by how easily and quickly a little girl talk can turn from innocent chit chat between friends into cruel gossip.

I'm pretty sure you would never want to be the victim of gossip so please remember how you would feel before you speak negatively about others.

An easy way to escape the trap of being a part of gossip is to always Speak P.I.N.K. (POSITIVE, IMPORTANT, NECESSARY, KIND)

Speak P.I.N.K.!

Lesson #12
Speak P.I.N.K.

Don't be a gossip girl! Nothing good comes from girls gossiping about one another. Saying things about others that you wouldn't say if they were in the room during the conversation is a hint that it's gossip and not innocent girl talk. Think about how you would want others to speak of you if you were not present. Listening to gossip puts you in an avoidable awkward situation to defend your character.

Listening to others who speak mean things about other girls can be just as unpleasant as actually speaking those mean words yourself. To disassociate yourself when those conversations begin can be as simple as saying something like, "I can't be a part of this conversation" or "I don't feel this is appropriate to talk about" or "I can not be associated with this" or ask "do you think it's fair to speak about someone who is not here to defend themselves?" Those statements can end the conversation, give you the opportunity to remove yourself or you may be totally ignored. The important thing is how you handle it.

When speaking, regardless of who is involved, speak positive. To determine the difference between innocent and fun *Girl Talk* and what is cruel gossip, ask yourself if it's **P.I.N.K.**

P.I.N.K.

Is it POSITIVE?
Is it IMPORTANT?
Is it NECESSARY?
Is it KIND?

Speak positive, important, necessary and kind. **(P.I.N.K.)** Like the old saying goes "If you don't have anything nice to say don't say anything at all."

A lot of reality television shows, celebrity reports, popular magazines, social blogs and in many cases our peers or families suggest that gossip is normal girl talk and innocent. That is not at all true. In fact often the consequences of gossip play out in front of us and in many cases the consequence is immediate and sometimes irreversible.

If we all spoke **P.I.N.K.** more often we could save ourselves lots of trouble, a lot of pain, regret and embarrassment.

The same people who would speak negative about others will speak negative about you when you are not around. Don't be a gossip girl, there is nothing **P.I.N.K.** about it.

Quiz #12

Speak P.I.N.K. stands for

A. pink, important, nosey, kind
B. pretty, impossible, necessary, know
C. positive, important, necessary, kind

When is it okay to gossip about others?

A. Always
B. Sometimes
C. Never

Listening to someone talking about others isn't gossip.   **TRUE** or **FALSE**

What type of responses would you give if someone began to gossip and expected you to join in? Explain.

_____
_____
_____
_____
_____
_____
_____

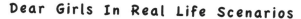

Dear Diary #12

Meet Demi who has a few new friends that love to gossip.
Demi wrote about it in her diary.

July 18th

Dear Diary,

I have been at my new school for about 3 months and it seems to be going well! I have a few friends and my teachers seem to be pretty cool. Marsha and Arlene are my best friends so far. They are really funny and like all the things I like.

Well it seems like every time we all get together they kinda talk about other girls that might not be really close with us.

Marsha sometimes says things like "Did you see Mindy's hair today?", and sometimes she laughs at Lisa when she reads out loud in class. Arlene on the other hand always talks about how everyone dresses and what kind of shoes they have on. They go on and on about

121

her stuff being so much better than everyone else. Uuuggghhhh! It's terrible!

They do this all the time and then ask me what do I think. I don't think anything. Those things are mean. Guess what? Well now a rumor is going around school. I will bet Marsha and Arlene started it and I do not want to be in any trouble and I don't want Marsha and Arlene to be mad at me but this is way too much for me. What should I do?

Love,

Demi

Dear Girls In Real Life Scenarios

Letter #12 Journal Entry

Demi is feeling the effects of gossip. Write to her she needs some advice.

Date _____

Dear Demi,

_____
_____
_____
_____
_____
_____
_____
_____
_____
_____
_____
_____
_____
_____
_____
_____
_____
_____
_____
_____

Love,

_____

Lesson #13

The Truth About Body Image

"The truth about body image is the beauty of imperfection belongs to us all."

Simeaka Melton

Dear Girls,

Seems like everywhere we turn, body image seems to be the center of discussion. Too skinny, too fat, too tall, too short, too dark, too light, freckles, no freckles, a big gap, no gap, hair, lips, butt, breasts, legs, feet, ugggghhh!

Don't believe the hype! Society constantly sends messages to fool you into believing that you are not enough. Why? If you knew you were already enough they wouldn't profit from your insecurities.

Do not compare yourself to others because the only image that matters is yours. Perfection is a lie.

The truth about body image is the beauty of imperfection belongs to us all.

Lesson #13
The Truth About Body Image

Girls are bombarded with distorted images of beauty everyday. It is no wonder the topic of body image has so many girls so uncomfortable with the way their bodies look. The media portrays unrealistic images and unrealistic expectations of beauty that no one can-and should not attempt-to achieve.

We were all made intentionally different, just like fingerprints. Unique, intentional and matchless. Our body types vary and no one is the same. Our shapes, sizes, colors, personalities, our overall image-everyone is different. In some cases we have similarities but still we are different. The things that make you different also make you special. Be sure to embrace your differences and do not try to erase them.

By using camera tricks, photo shop, and various tools, oftentimes images seen on television, magazines, billboards and other media outlets show the illusion of perfection. The truth about body image is the beauty of imperfection belongs to all of us. Perfection is a lie that does not exist.

Nothing and no one is perfect. So love the body you have been gifted.

Simeaka Melton

SIX Keys
To Loving Your Body

1. **Our bodies are made like fingerprints.**
Unique. Matchless. Irreplaceable. Unable to be duplicated.

2. **Do not compare yourself to others.**
Comparing yourself to others is pointless. You are who you are so there is no need to attempt to be someone you were born not to be.

3. **Focus on the things your love about body.**
Embrace the things that make you unique. If you are lucky enough not to blend in, do not try to, enjoy it!

4. **Celebrate yourself always.**
Do not put yourself down. Your words

128

have power. If you speak down you will feel down. Do not wait for others to compliment you. Celebrate yourself always.

5. **Dress age and body appropriate.**

Dress in clothing that fits your body well and that also suits your age. Too tight, too lose or too old, does not highlight your beauty.

6. **Treat your body right. A healthy body is a happy body.**

Exercise to be healthy and never to look like magazine images or anyone else. Balanced meals are key! Eat well, healthy and daily.

Simeaka Melton

Quiz #13

The truth about body image is

A. imperfection only exist in some girls
B. the beauty of imperfection belong to all of us
C. being perfect is beautiful

Embrace your differences

A. Always
B. Sometimes
C. Never

The media portray unrealistic images and expectations of beauty.

TRUE or **FALSE**

Explain how the way body image is portrayed in the media, magazines or reality television make you feel.

_____
_____
_____
_____
_____
_____
_____

130

Dear Girls In Real Life Scenarios

Dear Diary #13

Meet Kim. Kim is new at school and what more than anything to fit in with the other girls. Kim wrote about it in her diary.

November 6th

Dear Diary,

I want more than anything to fit in with the girls in my new school. Because I'm shorter, smaller, thinner and my voice is kinda like a baby it's so hard to fit in.

This weekend I'm going to give myself a makeover. I have a bunch of magazines for great ideas. I am ready! I can't wait to get started.

Here's what I'm going to do! I'm going to color pieces of my hair, pink, blue, yellow and green. I think it looks silly but the girls have their hair like that and they seem to think it's cool. I'm going to wear more green. Green seems to be everyone's favorite color but I like yellow best. I'm going to paint my nails a different color every day. I don't know why they do that but I will try it. And last thing I'm not going to be seen reading a book in public.

I love to read all the time but I never see the girls reading, only listening to music. I think that will do it!

Love,

Kim

Dear Girls In Real Life Scenarios

Letter #13 Journal Entry

What do you think about Kim's make over? Write a letter to let her know what you think.

Date _____

Dear Kim,

_____
_____
_____
_____
_____
_____
_____
_____
_____
_____
_____
_____
_____
_____
_____
_____
_____
_____
_____
_____
_____
_____

Love,

_____

Lesson #14

The Big Deal About Hair

"Good hair is your hair."
Simeaka Melton

Dear Girls,

Hair. Hair. Hair. Oh my! We can go on and on about our hair. Kinky hair. Curly hair. Straight hair. Coily hair, wavy hair, bushy hair, locked hair. Long, short, brown, red, black, blonde. Wow, the list is endless.

Seems like we always want the hair we do not have. Hair can be defined a lot of ways but hair does not define you. Hair can be fun but it is not important.

If you happen to have hair, don't glorify or worry about your hair. It's only hair. There are so so so so many more important things in the world. You are so much more than your hair so don't make it a big deal.

Lesson #14

The Big Deal About Hair

Hair! Hair! Hair! Have you ever wondered why hair is such a big deal for girls? Hair is made to be a big deal when girls are tricked into believing that there is something wrong with their hair differences.

There is so much beauty in our differences. No matter if you have kinky hair, curly hair, braided hair, straight hair, wavy hair, bushy hair or locked hair, love your hair no matter what hair you have!

Don't feel bad about your hair because it may be different than someone else's! If your hair is long, short, brown, red, black, blonde, polka dot or striped, whatever your hair is, do not allow anyone to make you feel bad about your hair. Knowing that beauty is found in our differences, we shouldn't make one another feel bad about our hair differences.

There is so much talk about good hair and bad hair. Chances are you have heard comments like "she has good hair" or "she has bad hair". There is no such thing as bad hair, only good hair. Good hair is your hair! Whatever hair someone has is good hair.

The most important purpose of hair is protection from things like sunlight, and other environmental dangers. So if you are blessed enough to have hair, have fun with your hair and do not worry about it.

Hair is no big deal so do not make others feel bad about their hair and do not be ashamed or feel bad about your own hair. It is perfectly fine to admire someone else's hair, but love your own hair. Do not wish you had hair you do not have. The hair you have is intentional.

Regardless whether it is bushy, wavy, twisted, braided, straight, curly, short, long, thick, thin or whatever, just have fun with it! It's no big deal, it's only hair.

Why is hair is such a big deal for girls?

A. Girls do not like hair and want to wear hats
B. Girls are tricked into believing that there is something wrong with their hair differences
C. Girls have too many hair options

Girls should feel bad about their hair when their hair is different than other girls.

A. Always
B. Sometimes
C. Never

It is perfectly fine to admire someone else's hair but love your own.

TRUE or FALSE

Explain a time when someone has made you feel bad about your hair.

_____
_____
_____
_____
_____
_____
_____
_____

*Meet Yolanda. Yolanda's hair worries has her down. You
may be able to relate. Look what she wrote in her diary.*

August 17th

Dear Diary,

I hate my hair! It won't do anything! It's short and kinky and brown and I just hate it. Gabby has nice curly hair. Amy has soft bouncy hair. Lee has silky straight hair. Viola's has fluffy ponytails. And Ashanti's braids are the best! Then there is me, a bird's nest!

I have the worse hair of them all! It wont do anything. Sometimes it's embarrassing and I wish I could wear a hat every day. My mom said I have hair so thick she can't do anything with it. My grandmother says my hair is just a big mess. I can't do anything about it I just want good hair like my friends.

Tomorrow we are taking group pictures at school and I have a

bird's nest for hair. Well maybe I
will wear a hat! Or just won't be
in the picture at all! Yeah I think
I will leave early so I don't have
to be in the pictures. I really hate
my hair! :(

Love,

Yolanda

Simeaka Melton

Letter #14 Journal Entry

Yolanda hates her hair. Write her a letter about how she is feeling.

Date _____

Dear Yolanda,

_____
_____
_____
_____
_____
_____
_____
_____
_____
_____
_____
_____
_____
_____
_____
_____
_____
_____
_____
_____
_____
_____

Love,

_____

Lesson #15

The Bad Touch

"No one ever deserves to be violated by a bad touch."

Simeaka Melton

Dear Girls,

Talks about good touch and bad touch could be a bit awkward but nevertheless it is very necessary to discuss. There is a good touch however do not be fooled because there is also a bad touch. A good touch is something that is kind, innocent, makes you feel loved and requires you to do nothing in return although your natural instinct may have you return the touch. Like a hug for a hug, a pat on the back, something as simple as that.

Touches that make you feel nervous or uncomfortable or scared are usually bad touches. A bad touch usually happens on the areas of your body that a one piece bathing suit covers. Those areas are your private areas. No one has the right to touch you in those areas.

Sometimes doctor visits may require you to be touched in those private areas when your parent or caregiver is present. For health reasons of course. Your parent or caregiver being present assists in making you appropriately comfortable.

If you have any questions or if someone has touched in an inappropriate way tell an adult you trust immediately. If that adult does not believe you tell someone else.

Never feel guilty or ashamed, and never keep it a secret. You have done nothing wrong. Find an adult you can trust until you get help.

Lesson #15

The Bad Touch

Is there is a good touch and bad touch? Yes, there are both touches.

A good touch usually comes from people who love and care about us, like your parents, siblings, friends or family. It could be a simple hug, pat on the head, or even handholding. A good touch makes us feel loved, comforted, happy or safe.

A bad touch is something that makes you feeling uncomfortable. A bad touch can also make you feel scared, guilty, nervous, confused, bad or even dirty. The person who gives the bad touch wants you to feel scared, guilty nervous or confused because they hope if you feel that way you will not tell anyone.

A bad touch is wrong and you should always tell someone. It is very important that you know you are NOT bad and you have not done anything wrong. If someone touches you in a bad way that person has done something bad and it is never your fault.

You may be surprised to learn that bad touches can come from an adult you may trust and care about, like a parent, sibling, family friends, family members. Even a teacher, coach, pastor, neighbor, and babysitter could possibly be people that would violate your trust with a bad touch.

Another concerning fact is women could also give girls and boys bad touches. Reports have been made of women touching girls and boys in bad ways, as well as reports of men touching boys and girls in bad ways.

A bad touch is a bad touch regardless of who touches. A bad touch can come from anyone. In any case, no matter the person doing the touching, a bad touch is never your fault and should never be a secret. Always tell someone to get help.

The person who gives the bad touch will try to trick or confuse you by saying things to scare you, hoping you will not tell anyone.

Here are **some** lies they might say:

- ✓ No one will believe you.
- ✓ You were bad.
- ✓ I didn't mean it.
- ✓ This was your fault.
- ✓ You asked for this.
- ✓ You tricked me.
- ✓ I thought you wanted this to happen.
- ✓ Look at what you made me do.
- ✓ I will kill your parents.
- ✓ I will go to jail.
- ✓ You will go to jail.
- ✓ Your mom will go to jail.
- ✓ Your dad will go to jail.
- ✓ I am the only one who loves you.
- ✓ No one will love you if they find out.
- ✓ No one will trust you.
- ✓ This is our secret.
- ✓ Your parents will be mad at you.
- ✓ You liked it.
- ✓ Why did you let me do it?
- ✓ You could have said no.
- ✓ You were a bad girl. That's why this happened.
- ✓ You don't want to make your parents mad, angry or sad.
- ✓ I will tell them you are lying and they will all hate you.

149

The list goes on and on. Do not ever believe the lies. There are so many lies the person will say to you to keep you silent and scared and confused. You do not need to be scared or feel guilty. It is never your fault and you can find help. Do not keep bad touch secrets to yourself.

The areas of your body that a one piece bathing suit covers are your private areas. No one has the right to touch you in those areas. The areas near your private areas, like your thighs, hips, or stomach should also not be touched. Your body belongs to you and you have the right to say no and the right tell if someone does not listen and the right to tell if you have been touched.

When your parents are present the doctor may need to examine such areas so be sure to discuss that with your parents or a trusted adult.

If you have been touched without permission near, in or on the areas of your body that are private or areas that a bathing suit would cover, or if you have any questions speak to an adult you trust immediately.

If your friend comes to you and tells you that someone has touched them in a bad way, listen, tell her or him that it is not their fault and encourage your friend to immediately tell an adult she or he trust.

Your friend may feel scared, guilty, ashamed, nervous, confused or even embarrassed. Just assure them that it is not their fault, they did nothing wrong and there is nothing to be ashamed about. It is possible that your friend will ask you to keep this secret. Your friend might say things like "You can't tell anyone", or "If you are truly my friend you wont tell" or "I don't want to get it in trouble" or "I don't want anyone to know".

Just explain that you have to get help because it's safest.

Once you explain that you must tell a trusted adult, your friend may become upset. Do not be surprised if your friend becomes angry and says things like "I thought I could trust you" or "I am never speaking to you ever again" or even "I hate you". It's okay and don't take it to heart because of all the emotions your friend may not be thinking rationally. Just do your part to do what's right. Your friend will thank you in the long run.

Above all, remember a bad touch will cause many different emotions but just know that no one deserves to be violated by a bad touch.

Resources For Help:

www.rainn.org   www.d2l.org   www.vicitimsofcrime.org

www.nsvrc.org   www.ncdsv.org   www.nnedv.org

A bad touch can come from

A. <u>Anyone</u>
B. A Tree
C. A Couch

If someone ever touches you in a bad way you should tell a trusted adult.

A. <u>Always</u>
B. Sometimes
C. Never

Being touched in a bad way is never your fault. The person who does the bad touch is at fault not the person who has been touched.

<u>TRUE</u> or **FALSE**

If your friend has been touched in a bad way what is something that you would say to her or him?

_____
_____
_____

Simeaka Melton

Dear Diary #15

Meet Jane Doe. Jane Doe wrote about the bad touch in her diary.

Dear Diary,

My uncle has been touching me and it makes me feel nasty and scared. I don't ask him to stop or why because I'm scared I will get in trouble. I hate the way he looks at me and I wish he would stop coming over.

I told my mother and she told me to shut up. My mother said she didn't want to hear any foolish talk and I should know better than that.

I told my grandfather and he said the men in the family know what they are doing I should appreciate the help. I don't even know what he means but he told me if he hears me speak of it again I was gonna get the worst punishment I have ever had. So I just don't say anything, I just let my uncle touch me.

Now I am really scared because
this weekend the kids have to stay
at my uncle's house and my uncle
said after all the kids go to sleep
he has a special surprise for me. I
told my mom I didn't want to go
and she said I had to go. WHAT AM
I GOING TO DO?!

Love,

Jane Doe

Dear Girls In Real Life Scenarios

Letter #15
Jane Doe needs help. Write her a letter to offer help.

Date _____

Dear Jane Doe,

_____
_____
_____
_____
_____
_____
_____
_____
_____
_____
_____
_____
_____
_____
_____
_____
_____
_____
_____
_____
_____

Love,

_____

157

Lesson #16

I Love M.U.S.I.C.

"Music is as necessary to life as a spoon is to soup!"

Simeaka Melton

Dear Girls,

I love music! I really really love music! Music makes me dance before I even know the words to the song! Music is life's universal language. Without exchanging words, music unites and connects people, making them smile, laugh, sing along, high five and of course dance!

I love good music because music sets the tone and adds an extra boost to the day.

When choosing music be mindful, understand, speak and invite only good positive energy into your heart. Be conscious because music matters to our souls!

Lesson #16

I Love M.U.S.I.C.

Music matters! Music makes us dance, makes us happy, gives us courage to sing silly songs in public, inspires us to conquer small fears, it makes us feel good about ourselves and even gives us confidence!

It has been said that music is like food to the soul. Just like with food we have to be careful what we eat. While some foods are good for us there are some foods that can make us sick. Well, music has sort of the same effect. As a result we have to be careful about what type of music we listen to because music does effects us. Depending on what type of music we choose to listen to, music has either a positive or negative effect.

There are so many genres of music to explore. Be sure to explore all types of music to enjoy the best music for the most fun to love. Regardless of the music that you decide to love, chose positive!

Here are a few tips to choosing music that is right for you.

M.U.S.I.C.

M.U.S.I.C.

Mindful
Understand
Speak
Intercept & Invite
Conscious

M Mindful

Mindful – To be careful

Be mindful of the words you speak.

Alert | Vigilant | Watchful | Knowledgeable

U Understand

Understand – Perceive the intended meaning of the words.

Understand what you are saying.

Comprehend| Realize| Apprehend | Grasp

S Speak

Speak – To express oneself. To make

known. To express thoughts.

The words you speak are making a request.

Declare | Expose| Proclaim | Reveal

I   Intercept and Invite

Intercept – to stop or block.

Cut Off| Block| Prevent | Interrupt

Invite – increase the likely hood, to request

Request| Ask| Offer | Urge

C   Conscious

Be aware of the intent behind the music lyrics. Conscious– mentally perceptive or alert

Aware | Alert| Conscious | Inwardly Attentive

The next time you're listening to music ask yourself if you can say,

"I Love M.U.S.I.C."

Quiz #16

We have to be careful what type of music we listen to because

A. music can be weird.
B. music has an effects on us.
C. music makes us hungry.

Be mindful of the type of music you listen to.

A. Always
B. Sometimes
C. Never

Music effects your mood.

TRUE or **FALSE**

What is your favorite song? Why?

_____
_____
_____
_____
_____
_____
_____
_____
_____
_____
_____

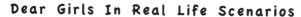

Dear Diary #16

Meet Erin. Erin and her friends are trying out for the talent show. Erin wrote about it in her diary.

June 9th

Dear Diary,

My friends and I have been practicing our dance routine for months and we finally have it just right! One problem. The music that we have been practicing to is kind of bad. Well not that bad but I overheard my Mom and Dad talking about how awful the song is and how they would never let me listen to such garbage. As a matter of fact, every time the song comes on the radio they turn quick!

We can't change the song because our dance routine won't be the same and I can't be the reason we might have any problems during the competition.

The winners get bikes and their picture in the newspaper. If I ask them to change the music it might cost us the competition.

What should I do? Uuugggghhhh!!!

> Love,
>
> Erin

Dear Girls In Real Life Scenarios

Letter #16

Erin is has a real dilemma. Write to her she needs some advice.

Date _____

Dear Erin,

_____
_____
_____
_____
_____
_____
_____
_____
_____
_____
_____
_____
_____
_____
_____
_____
_____
_____
_____
_____
_____
_____

Love,

_____

Lesson #17

Pretty Girl Pressure

"The pretty girl pressure is the pressure to achieve pretty as only society defines and approves it. All girls and women have the power to eliminate the pretty girl pressure if we choose."

Simeaka Melton

Dear Girls,

You are so beautiful! You are beautiful on your worst days, you are beautiful on bad days, you are beautiful when others intentionally make you feel like you are not and you are still beautiful when someone else beautiful stands next to you.

Don't ever ask for permission to be comfortable in your beauty. Our unique imperfections make us individually beautiful. Make it known that you embrace them without shame. Own your beauty, love it and share it with others.

So many girls feel the pressure to achieve the validation of others opinion of "Yes, she's pretty". You are more than pretty, you are beautiful! You must recognize that without pressure and without comparison and without permission or validation.

Believe in the beauty that you are and do not seek the illusion of pretty.

P.S.
Be Beautiful, inside and out!
Don't fall for the pretty girl pressure.

Lesson #17

Pretty Girl Pressure

Take a moment and repeat these words.

I am beautiful.
I am beautiful.
I am beautiful.
And I am certainly enough,
as I am.

You are so beautiful! You are beautiful when you feel ugly. You are beautiful when someone says you are not. You are beautiful when someone else beautiful stands next to you. You are beautiful when you are having a bad day. You are beautiful when you see someone beautiful in magazines. You are beautiful when you think you are not. You are beautiful. Always beautiful.

Beauty is something we are all born with and not something we have to achieve. Too often society dismisses and undervalues authentic beauty by simply replacing it with the desire to achieve pretty. As a result, girls often do not recognize or understand or want their true beauty so they attempt to achieve "pretty" as society has defined it.

Who is society?

Society is the general public, the culture

that we all live in and an established way of life from groups of people.

What is the pretty girl pressure?

The pretty girl pressure is the pressure to achieve pretty, as society unrealistically defines it.

Whenever you feel the pressure of the following:

inappropriate diets, push up bras, padded bras, plastic surgery, obsession with make-up, sexy clothing, validation from others, eating disorders, negative self talk, comparing yourself to other girls, the desperate need to have the things other girls have, attempts to imitate what's seen on television or in magazines, self shame about your outer appearance, risky behaviors to fit in, the unrealistic idea that you can be flawless or perfect, the list goes on and on, **the pretty girl pressure is in full effect.**

As a result, lowered self esteem is a major side effects of pretty girl pressure.

How are girls tricked into pretty girl pressure?

Girls are tricked into the pretty girl pressure by society. Society unrealistically defines pretty as something exclusive and attainable by only a chosen group of girls and women they have approved.

Society tells us the toxic untruth that pretty is something girls must achieve. The simple truth is, you are naturally beautiful. When girls have the desire to achieve what they believe only some girls are able to achieve, the pretty girl pressure begins.

What are the effects of the pretty girl pressure?

FACTS: Media Influence and The Effects On Self Image

- 9 out of 10 girls feel pressure by the fashion and media industries to be skinny
- Over 60% of girls compare themselves to fashion models
- 69% of girls in 5th - 12th grade report that magazine pictures influence their idea of the perfect body shape
- 70% of 6 – 12 year olds want to be thinner
- Between 5th – 9th grade, girls hide their accomplishments perceiving that being smart isn't sexy
- 90% of eating disorders are found in girls

Sources: National Eating Disorder Association, National Association of Anorexia, Education.com, NYU Child Study Center, Park Nicollet Melrose Center and National Association of Self Esteem

The beauty industry is a multi billion dollar industry and if WE already knew we were beautiful perhaps the industry would not profit so much from our insecurities.

It's okay to get glammed up from time to time and actually can be pretty fun. It's also perfectly okay not to get glammed up at all. *"Glammed Up"* as in those things like make up, hair, nails, shoes, bows, clothes, fashion accessories and other glammy things we enjoy. Regardless, you must remember those glammy things are for fun and not necessities and does NOT create beauty.

Think about this. The Webster's Dictionary definition of the word ***pretty*** *is attractive in a delicate way without being truly beautiful.*
With that in mind, here are words of wisdom.

Don't fall for the pretty girl pressure.
Eliminate it by activating your girl power and being beautiful, inside and out!

Society unrealistically defines pretty as

A. something funny.
B. something exclusive.
C. something weird.

I recognize my true beauty.

A. Always
B. Sometimes
C. Never

It's important to me to be pretty.

TRUE or **FALSE**

Explain your answer.

_____

_____

_____

_____

_____

_____

_____

_____

_____

_____

_____

Do you feel the pretty girl pressure? Explain your answer.

_____
_____
_____
_____
_____
_____
_____
_____
_____
_____
_____
_____
_____
_____
_____
_____
_____
_____
_____

Dear Diary #17
Meet Phoebe. Phoebe really cares about being pretty.
Phoebe wrote all about it in her diary.

September 18th

Dear Diary,

People always tell me how pretty I am. I AM PRETTY! :) I am going to be a model! I am so much prettier than my friends too. They just don't cut it. Since I am always looking through fashion and style magazines I try to keep them up to date on the trends and what's in style and cool to help them out. All the glam in the magazines inspire me to be just like the models. Pretty and fabulous!

Sometimes it can feel like a lot of pressure trying to be so pretty all the time but beauty is pain right! Right! So if I skip a couple of meals to stay fit it's for a good cause. Pretty! lol :) And staying home because I'm having a bad hair day is a must!

The girls in the magazine are always perfect. Hair! Nails! Clothes! Make-Up!

Sooooooo many accessories! Man what a life! I'm already pretty but when I grow up I am really going to be prettier than ever and famous and rich! Whelp gotta go get pretty! :)

Love,

Phoebe

Dear Girls In Real Life Scenarios

Letter #17

Phoebe has a lot of ideas about pretty. Write to her a letter about what she thinks

Date _____

Dear Phoebe,

_____

_____

_____

_____

_____

_____

_____

_____

_____

_____

_____

_____

_____

_____

_____

_____

_____

_____

_____

_____

_____

_____

Love,

_____

Lesson #18

The Facts Of Life

"We never know it all but the older we get the more facts of life we discover."

Simeaka Melton

Dear Girls,

The older you get, the more you will learn along your journey. The facts of life do not change. You can learn a lot from the older generations as they begin to converse about their journeys. Whenever you hear a group of women having a little girl talk about their lives as young girls, pay close attention when you hear statements that begins with "If I only knew then ....." or "If I had only known ...." or "oh how I remember", those are all statements that have alot of wisdom, experience of error and something that the older folk call "hind sight".

The facts of life do not change just pay attention as you do.

Lesson #18

The Facts Of Life

There are countless facts of life. Nearly every woman can begin a sentence with "If I only knew then what I know now ...."

We never know it all but the older we get the more facts of life we discover. Life is like a huge classroom with endless lessons. If you pay attention to what is happening around you, you will be surprised by the many lessons life has to offer.

You will make mistakes, you will lose friends, you will have disappointments and you will even go through and live through things that are unfair and you cannot control them. The great news is you will also have wonderful and fabulous and fun things that happen in your life. You will experience happiness, you will have plenty of victories, accomplish great things, be the reason someone smiles, you will have plenty to things to make you laugh aloud and you will do amazing things in this world.

There are good parts and there are bad parts of life, there are also easy parts and hard parts of life, and a lot of little details in between, otherwise known as the **"cards you are dealt"**.

No one can control the cards they are dealt but you can control how you respond and react to what life deals you.

An important fact of life is to always remember that everyone has a story. Everyone. Never judge others by their story and do not be embarrassed by your story. Your story does not define you it explains you. Don't get stuck in the rough parts of your story. Your life is like a canvas, gifted especially for you, so paint it anyway you please, as longs as it reflects the best of you.

There is no such thing as a life better than yours, let your life produce greatness.

Everyday is an opportunity to learn something new or experience something new or share something new.

In this chapter you will find are a few simple facts of life to help you in your journey.

The Facts Of Life

1. Appreciate every breath your take.

Life is short and in a split second life can change. Therefore do not take it for granted, always appreciate life. You are alive on purpose so act like it. Appreciate every breath you take.

2. Pay it forward.

Service to others is the privilege of life and the freedom of acts of kindness has its own reward. Share the good in your life with others. Service to others is an excellent way to pay it forward.

3. Respect your elders.

Your elders deserve respect merely by the laws of nature. We walk in their path and if we listen we will find immeasurable wisdom. Your elders have history unexplained and often unacknowledged in history books. Respect your elders, who have blazed the trails you have the privilege of walking.

4. Be the bigger person.
Some things do not require a response. In many cases having the last word is often pointless and often causes conflict, not resolution. Some things do not warrant a response. Speak with intent and pick your battles wisely.

5. Work hard.
You must work hard for whatever you want to achieve. Nothing about achieving your dreams is easy. Hard work prepares for the success you plan. There are no short cuts to hard work. You must simple work hard.

6. Dream Big.
Do not let anyone convince you that you can not achieve your dreams and goals.

Avoid sharing your big dreams with small minded people. Dream bigger than others say you can, then plan accordingly.

7. Education matters.

Your education is something no one can ever take from you. A strong educational foundation will set you apart from your peers, allowing you the opportunities to achieve your dreams on an upward level of excellence. Nevertheless do not rely solely of school for your education. Although your education begins in school and books, your education is capable of going beyond the traditional limits.

8. The company you keep matters at every age.

Birds of a feather flock together. You can not soar high like an eagle if you spend your time with playing chickens. Surround yourself with like minded people. Those who encourage you to do and be your best and also those you can encourage to do their best.

9. Broken hearts heal.

Many things will break your heart. From boys, friends, life's disappointments and things you will learn along your journey. Something will break your heart at one time or other BUT you will survive. Keep your head up and keep moving forward because broken hearts heal.

10. The world owes you nothing.

Regardless of your circumstances and regardless of the cards you've been dealt the world owes you nothing. You must allow your disappointments and pain to produce power in your life. There is purpose in your pain so be the change you want to see.

11. Forgiveness

Forgiveness is the key to peace at heart. Don't focus on the fault but remember you too have also been forgiven for your faults. Unforgiving is something that hurts you. Anytime you decide not to forgive, you decide to be angry. Anytime you are angry, you make the decision to upset your peace. To complete your joy you must forgive. Forgive because you to have been forgiven.

12. You are worthy.

You are worth love, respect, greatness and all the joys the world has to offer. You are priceless. Don't sell yourself short by behaving less than what you deserve.

13. Don't be a Bag Lady.

Having guilt, shame, anger, resentment, bitterness, hate, fear, depression, embarrassment, loneliness, all the things that decrease your self esteem and self view are known as the **Bag Lady** syndrome. Taking ownership of things that decreases you will eventually destroy your self esteem if you do not seek help.

You are not your circumstance.
Regardless of what happens in your life you are still worthy and loved. Don't be a **Bag Lady** seek help from a trusted adult or counselor. We all can use help sorting the baggage we carry.

14. Life is to be celebrated.

Celebrate life by spreading the love everywhere you go because you only get one life. Enjoy with the attitude of gratitude. Also remember not to rely on others to celebrate you. Celebrate yourself and the life you have been gifted. Life is to be celebrated regardless of the circumstances.

15. Have an honorable reputation.

A bad reputation is like a disease ... hard to get rid of. People will judge you by your reputation, so do what's right. Treat others the way you would like to be treated and respect yourself.

16. Keep your word.

Your word should be stronger than oak. When you say you are going to do something, do it. No excuses. Make sure your word is something people can trust. Be honorable by your word. Do not over commit and do not agree as an emotional promise. If you are ever not able to keep your word you must be upfront and honest. That makes it a bit more understandable because it's not a habit.

17. Say 'I love you' as often as you can.

Regardless of what people may say, they love to hear the words "I love you". The same feeling you get when your loved ones tells you how much they love you is the same feeling the people you care about get when you tell them you love them. People need to know, feel and hear "I love you". Say "I love you" as often as you can.

18. Live life rising above expectations.

Dream as big as you can imagine and do the unexpected. Nowadays expectations are set pretty low for young girls. **Live life rising above expectations** because your reality is what you create not what you are told.

19. You are worth the wait.

Don't let boys pressure you into things you are not ready for because you are worth the wait. Sex is ideally an exclusive act between married people and when you step outside of that you enter a world mentally, spiritually and emotionally you are not equipped to handle. You are worth the wait.

20. Don't get stuck in your story.

Everyone has a story. There is no such thing as a life better than yours. Your story does not define you it explains you. Don't get stuck in your story.

21. Listen more than you talk.

You learn so much when you listen. There is a time to listen and a time to talk. Learn the difference.

22. Create your own reality.

Someone else's perception does not have to be your reality. Often times, young girls are judged on many untruths. Do not allow someone else's perception determine how you create your reality. Create your reality of truth and honor.

23. Put on your big girl panties.

Don't avoid difficult situations. **Put on your big girl panties** is an old saying that means deal with the difficult situations in life. Avoiding the difficult things in life only slows down your progress.

24. Use your imagination.

Being average is unacceptable. Use your natural creativity and imagination to think outside the box. Your individual creativity is your vehicle to setting you apart in your talent.

25. Do what's right.

Always do what's right. Make decisions in integrity, purpose, perseverance and love. Although you may not always want to, and sometime it may not be popular BUT the time is always right to do what's right.

26. Write the vision.

Writing your vision in your own handwriting is another way for you to see the possibility of the life you desire. You must write your vision in plain English because if there isn't a written vision there isn't a plan to accomplish the life you desire (your dream).

Envisioning the life you desire is vital because when YOU are able to imagine your possibilities for yourself, disappointments and hurdles will not easily discourage you. Envisioning the life you desire motivates you to refuse defeat and achieve your vision. You must constantly envision the life you desire.

Working hard to achieve the life you does not happen by occasional attempts of working hard. You must constantly do things that prepare you for the life you desire. Educate yourself, practice the things you love and stay focused on what you enjoy.

27. Prioritize.

Life is full of fun stuff! Life is also full of opportunities and reasons to celebrate. Don't forget to prioritize. Doing what's necessary before you do what's popular will help you prioritize.

28. Take care of yourself.

As young women the older you get the more instinctive it may become to take care of others first or even to take care of others better than you take care of yourself. You must know you are required to take care of yourself just as you would your very best friend. When you love yourself you are able to truly love others. Take care of yourself first so you can take care of others.

29. Do your research.

It's not enough to take someone's word for it. Beware of the information that you accept for factual. Doing your own research allows you the benefit of being not only confident but also educated on the things you speak about and believe.

30. Stop. Think. Go.

Think before you speak. Think before you do things. Think before you post to social media. People may not remember exactly what you say but they will remember how you make them feel. Your actions are reflections of your character.

31. Keep Your Faith.

The world will sell you many things that may shake or shatter your faith. If you have faith as small as a mustard seed, you will be able to persevere through life's challenges. When you are rooted and grounded in the Word of God your faith reveals true and strength. Know that everything about your life is intentional.

32. Tell the truth.

Telling the truth isn't always easy but it is necessary. Lying only leads to heartache, guilt and anger. Although sometimes the truth can hurt feelings as well, if you tell the truth you have nothing to hide or cover up. You will have a light heart and it keeps you trustworthy. Do what's right and always tell the truth. When you do tell the truth you will have nothing to worry your mind or heart.

33. Sisterhood is good for the soul.

There are good friends, great friends and sister friends. When you are fortunate enough to have a sister friend or a few sister friends you are blessed. When you have sister friends that you can trust, laugh and cry with, encourage one another to be your best selves, while celebrating one another's achievements, have fun with and share kindness, you have truly found sisterhood. Protect your sisterhood with trust, honor, truth, support and love.

34. Old fashion girls rock.

Old fashion is so underrated! The "old fashion" treasures of our elders have impacted our lives, made our lives comfortable, and made our hearts smile. From things like homemade cooking and baking, to the many creations of sewing and knitting, and especially the perfect home remedies to add relief to our lives for generations.

As the old saying goes "Girls are made of sugar and spice and everything nice." So in other words be mindful of how we represent the integrity of being girls and later women. Compassion and love for others, be well-groomed, hygienically and health consciousness, and of course respect for yourself and others. Old fashion never gets old, it only rocks more as time goes on!

35. R-E-S-P-E-C-T goes a long way.

Treat people with the same respect you would want them to give the person you love the most. No one person is more worthy of respect than another person. Greet the school janitor with the same enthusiasm and respect you give the principal. Everyone you come in contact with, even for a brief moment, should have one more reason to smile. Make eye contact, give a simple hello, perhaps a smile, and a kind word or even two wouldn't hurt. You never know, something so small could be so big to someone.

36. Don't be a gossip girl.

Nothing good ever comes from gossip. Gossip always comes back to bite you in the end. Speak P.I.N.K (Positive, Important, Necessary and Kind) and be gossip free.

37. You are enough.

You are enough. You are enough as you are. You have nothing to prove and no reason to compare yourself to others. You are not only good enough you are great enough. You are enough just by the fact you have been born. Be proud.

38. Be D.O.P.E.

DEAL ONLY IN POSITIVE ENGERY. The less negativity and foolery you tolerate in your space the greater you become. Be D.O.P.E.

39. Do what you love.

Do the things you love. Even when others think it's pointless, means little, or finds reasons you should do something else. Do what you love because those things are what help build your dreams.

40. Love yourself.

Only when you love yourself will you be able to love others. Love your imperfections, your strengths, your differences, and even your quirkiness. You are wonderfully and fearfully made with love so love yourself and then enjoy loving others.

41. There is purpose in your pain.

Whatever the pain you experience just know there is purpose in your pain. Let your pain produce power in your life. Use those painful experiences for greater things intended.

42. Don't wait until tomorrow.

Procrastination is a state of mind and is a clear sign of your commitment to your task. Nothing you want will come to you, you must go out and get it. Be ready for opportunities when they arrive by avoiding procrastination. Take the initiative to do more than expected. Remember to have balance. Do the things that you are able to do when you are able to do. Why wait until tomorrow, when tomorrow may not come or your opportunity could be missed?

43. Accept the compliment.

You may be a girl or know of a girl who sometimes has a hard time accepting compliments. Accepting compliments are good for you and your self esteem. Example: If someone says to you "I like your dress, you look really pretty today" avoid saying something like "Oh I had this dress for a long time but okay". To accept a compliment with a simply "Thank you" is far better than brushing it off with an explanation. A simple thank you shows that you agree, recognize and believe that you are worthy. To brush off compliments demonstrates that you may be feeling less than worthy.

44. Different Strokes.

There are different strokes for different folks. Don't judge. Some folks will have a different way of doing things than you do. Don't let that distract you. Follow your own path, and do not judge others for theirs.

45. Your soul writes.

Writing is an expression of self. Journaling is empowering, soothing and creative. Something very powerful happens when you get to a quiet place, with yourself and use your mind freely to write. When you journal your soul writes.

46. Stay in your lane.

Don't let what other people do distract you from what you are supposed to do. Do not try to out do other people by doing what they do well. Don't get distracted by watching the people watching you. Stay in your lane.

47. The little things matter.

Pay attention to the little details because they matter.

Think.

Think about the effect you have on others. Using words like please, thank you, excuse me, and listening when others need it, has a special effect.

Speak.

Speak when you enter a room, encourage others without request, and speak **P.I.N.K.** about others.

Write.

Write thank you notes for gifts, acts of kindness received or exchange of time, or even write just because.

48. Embrace your differences.

We all have some things that make us different than others. Embrace your differences. The things that make us stand out make us special so don't attempt to blend in. Unapologetically stand out.

49. Agree with yourself.

Sometimes you just have to give yourself permission to agree with yourself. Look in the mirror and affirm yourself. Speak things into existence by using language like "I can _____ because I said so", I will _____ because I said so", I am _____ because I said so". The opinions of others do not matter so give yourself permission to agree with yourself.

50. Know your responsibility.

You are responsible for no one other than yourself. When you care about others sometimes you may feel like you are responsible to fix their situation. Remember you are responsible to be a good friend, and you are not responsible for their situation.

51. Activate your girl power.

Activate your girl power everyday. Activating your girl power begins in the freedom to be yourself without intentionally shrinking when other girls activate their girl power. Your girl power is your self love, your self confidence, your freedom to be your unique self and the ability to stretch yourself enough to excel in the things you do well. There is no power like girl power. Never ever give it away.

52. Refuse defeat.

It's not always easy but don't give up on yourself. Sometimes you have to encourage yourself but don't give up. Refuse defeat.

Dear G.I.R.L.S.

A Love Letter

From The Author

Dear Girls,

I have written this book for all girls under the sky! All Brown, Black, Tan, White, Latino, Biracial, Asian, Indian, Polka Dot, Paisley, and Striped. This book is for ALL beautiful girls under the sky.

It is my goal that you find this book, along with my included love letters, as a guide to activate your Girl Power. There is no power like Girl Power, never ever give it away, because with it you can change the world.

When the world attempts to trick you, remember to live life rising above expectations because you are worth your purpose.

You are enough to be the change you deserve to see.

Love Always,
Miss Meaka

SISTERHOOD
Affirmation

Dear Girls In Real Life Scenarios

The Sisterhood Affirmation

I am worth my purpose and so are you.

When you are down I will lift you up.

When you are afraid I will hold your hand.

I have your back knowing you also have mine.

Together we rise, divided we fall.

As sisters we stand to conquer the world.

We stand in integrity, purpose, perseverance and love.

We live life rising above expectations.

Quiz

Girls In Real Life Scenarios

Dear Girls In Real Life Scenarios

Dear G.I.R.L.S. Quiz Question #1
friends Or friendEmemies

You and your best friend had a disagreement and have not spoken in 3 days. Today in the school cafeteria you notice a group of girls making fun of her and she is clearly upset. What would you do?

A. Ignore it. You're not speaking to her.
B. Join in with the other girls.
C. Stand up for your friend.

Dear G.I.R.L.S. Quiz Question #2
Picture Day

It's school spirit week! You love spirit week because everyone gets involved. It's pajama day ... or so you thought. Today you have on your favorite pajamas. When you get to school you notice that everyone is dressed up in regular clothes. Oh no, it's picture day not pajamas day. What do you do?

A. Immediately go to the office and ask to call your parent.
B. Keep on your pajamas and take your picture anyway.
C. Go to the nurse and ask to go home sick.

Dear G.I.R.L.S. Quiz Question #3
Dance Team Dreams

You have a reputation of not being able to keep a secret. You have been challenged by your friends to not gossip and not to tell secrets for 2 weeks. It's only day nine and you just found out that there is a pop quiz in 3 days. If you and your friends don't get a good grade you won't be able to try out for the dance team. What do you do?

A. Lose the challenge and let everyone know there is a pop quiz coming up.
B. Offer to study together so you all can be prepared.
C. Ask your teacher to change the pop quiz until after the dance team tryouts.

Dear G.I.R.L.S. Quiz Question #4
Mrs. Weatherly

Your teacher, Mrs. Weatherly is explaining a difficult math equation to you but all you can do is try to avoid looking at her nose. Mrs. Weatherly has a huge booger in her nose and you are grossed out. What do you do?

A. Try to get through it without making a weird face.
B. Tell your friend about Mrs. Weatherly's nose.
C. Tell Mrs. Weatherly that she has something in her nose.

Dear Girls In Real Life Scenarios

Dear G.I.R.L.S. Quiz Question #5
The Secret

You just found out that Susan told your secret and now everyone knows you have a tutor. Kids are asking you questions about your tutor. What do you do?

A. Say it's not true, it's no one's business.
B. Tell Susan she has a big mouth and tell one of her secrets.
C. Own up to it, it's nothing to be ashamed of.

Dear G.I.R.L.S. Quiz Question #6
Time To Party

Sarah has been planning her birthday for weeks. You offered to make cupcakes and to come early to help her get set up. She is super excited. Uh-oh, Latia has just decided to have a party on the same night. She invited you to come. Gavin, who you have a major crush on, will also be there. What do you do?

A. Drop off the cupcakes to Sarah and go to Latia's party instead.
B. Tell Latia you can't make it. Maybe next time.
C. Leave Sarah's party early and go to Latia's party late.

Simeaka Melton

Dear G.I.R.L.S. Quiz Question #7
The Hair Cut

You are having a really good time at Janet's pajama party. Cindy says her mom is a hair stylist and then Cindy offers give all the girls bangs!

Cindy has cut four girls' bangs so far and you are next. As Cindy cuts your bangs you hear someone gasp! Next you hear someone say "oh no!". You immediately go to the mirror to look and your bangs are really short and horrible. You turned to Cindy and she has a smirk. She says "Oh well, it will grow back before you know it." Some girls have a shocked look on their faces other girls were shaking their heads. What do you do?

A. Cry and ask to go home.
B. Take the scissors from Cindy and cut her bangs just like she cut yours.
C. Even though you are mad, shake it off and brush your hair into a ponytail.

Dear G.I.R.L.S. Quiz Question #8
I Like Him Too

You and your friend Jasmine like the same boy from your class. His name is Darrell and he is really cute! Today at lunch he passed you a note, asking you to go to the school dance with him. What do you do?

A. Say yes! This is your big chance.
B. Say no because you don't want to hurt Keisha's feelings?
C. Ask Keshia how she would feel if you went to the dance with Darrell.

Dear G.I.R.L.S. Quiz Question #9
The Huge Mess

You're at Kim's party and Hunter, who you have a super crush on comes over to you and say you look really pretty. OMG! You immediately start to smile and as you walk away you trip and fall into the table, making a huge mess. Broken glass, juice, cups, and chips are everywhere. What do you do?

A. Cry and leave the party area.
B. Ask Hunter to help you clean it up.
C. Blame it on someone else.

Dear G.I.R.L.S. Quiz Question #10
Magazine Blues

You love looking at fashion and style magazines. Your favorite one is *Sparkle and Glam* Magazine. You believe the girls in the magazines are all so gorgeous and they seem to be picture perfect and so happy. Sometimes you feel bad about yourself when you look through the magazine because you don't look anything like the girls seen in the pictures. *Sparkle and Glam* Magazine has the best style tips but their pictures of all those gorgeous girls make you feel the worst. What do you do?

A. Stop looking through the magazines; it's not worth sad feelings.

B. Do something about the way you look. The girls in the magazines work hard to be gorgeous so do whatever they do.

C. Love yourself and your body and stop comparing yourself to what you see in magazines because you are enough as you are.

Dear Girls In Real Life Scenarios

Trivia

Girls In Real Life Scenarios

Dear G.I.R.L.S. Trivia Question #1

On a quiet rainy day what would you like to do most?

A. Read or write
B. Bake something
C. Talk on the phone
D. Watch television

Dear G.I.R.L.S. Trivia Question #2

Complete this sentence.

I am amazing because _____

_____

_____

_____.

Dear G.I.R.L.S. Trivia Question #3

What type of movie would you rather watch?

A. Comedy
B. Musical
C. Scary
D. Drama

Dear G.I.R.L.S. Trivia Question #4

What type of shoes would you pick to wear with your favorite fun dress?

A. Sneakers
B. Flip Flops
C. Sandals
D. Sparkle Party Shoes

Dear G.I.R.L.S. Trivia Question #5

If you could change one thing in the world what would it be? Explain the reason for your change?

_____

_____

_____

_____

_____

_____

_____

_____

_____

_____

_____

_____

Dear G.I.R.L.S. Trivia Question #6

If you were class President what would you do for the students and why?

_____

_____

_____

_____

_____

_____

_____

_____

_____

Dear G.I.R.L.S. Trivia Question #7

Why should you think twice before you post pictures or words to social media?

_____

_____

_____

_____

_____

_____

_____

Dear G.I.R.L.S. Trivia Question #8

Explain your personal fashion style.

_____

_____

_____

_____

_____

_____

_____

_____

_____

_____

Dear G.I.R.L.S. Trivia Question #9

What career do you want to have and how will you work to achieve your career goal?

_____

_____

_____

_____

_____

_____

_____

_____

Dear G.I.R.L.S. Trivia Question #10

Name six women you admire and why.

#1_____

Reason

_____

_____

_____

_____

#2 _____

Reason

_____

_____

_____

_____

#3 _____

Reason

_____

_____

_____

_____

Dear Girls In Real Life Scenarios

#4 _____

Reason

_____

_____

_____

_____

#5 _____

Reason

_____

_____

_____

_____

#6 _____

Reason

_____

_____

_____

_____

Diary

Girls In Real Life Scenarios

Dear Diary #1

Meet Samone. She's a history wiz! Samone wrote about it in her diary.

March 7th

Dear Diary,

Even though I love History I am starting to hate going to History class. I have always gotten straight A's in history and I seem to surprise all of my teachers with how much I know. Now here's the problem.

Some of the kids, actually a lot of the kids, well it feels like all of the kids make fun of me. Whenever my teacher, Ms. Carter ask me a question I know the answer. Whatever history question he asks I know the answer.

I can't help it! I love to read, I love history, I love to research, I love learning and I love talking about history. BUT I don't love history class!

The class teases me everyday.
Saying I'm a history brain, or
calling me the wiz kid or a little
miss know-it-all! It hurts my
feelings alot because they don't
want to work with me and never
invite me to their study groups. I
wish I wasn't so smart! Ummmmm
maybe I will just stop answering
questions.

Love,

Samone

Dear Girls In Real Life Scenarios

Letter #1

Samone is longer enjoying the whiz of history! Write a letter to Samone about how she is feeling.

Date _____

Dear Samone,

_____

_____

_____

_____

_____

_____

_____

_____

_____

_____

_____

_____

_____

_____

_____

_____

_____

_____

Love,

_____

231

Dear Diary #2

Meet Brooke. She has just had the most embarrassing moment yet. She wrote about it in her diary.

September 23rd

Dear Diary,

Guess what happened today? At lunch I sat in chocolate and of course I had no idea until I was walking down the hall and Peter yells out "she pooped herself!" and everyone started laughing. Uggghhh! Talk about embarrassed! Was I ever!!! Here's the thing. Peter and I just started going out 3 days ago and that was so rude! Maybe he didn't mean to hurt my feelings, maybe he did, maybe he didn't care. What should I do? Maybe there isn't anything to do. I don't' know. Help!

Love,

Brooke

Dear Girls In Real Life Scenarios

Letter #2

Brooke seems to be feeling a bit confused. Write a letter to
Brooke about how she is feeling.

Date _____

Dear Brooke,

_____
_____
_____
_____
_____
_____
_____
_____
_____
_____
_____
_____
_____
_____
_____
_____
_____
_____
_____
_____

Love,

_____

Dear Diary #3

Meet Lydia. She has good news. Lydia wrote about it in her diary.

May 5th

Dear Diary,

Today Coach Ryans posted the list of girls who made the cheerleading squad! And I made it! YES! YES! YES! I was the only one of my friends who made the squad! I don't want to come off like I'm bragging so I made out like it was no big deal because I don't want my friends to be mad at me. I'm wondering if it's okay to celebrate my good news or should I just keep it to myself. Who should I tell?

Love,

Lydia

Dear Girls In Real Life Scenarios

Letter #3

Lydia needs some advice. Write a letter to Lydia about how she is feeling maybe you can help.

Date _____

Dear Lydia,

_____

_____

_____

_____

_____

_____

_____

_____

_____

_____

_____

_____

_____

_____

_____

_____

_____

_____

_____

_____

Love,

_____

Dear Diary #4

Meet Tabatha. Tabatha has a note and she wrote about it in her diary.

August 8th

Dear Diary,

We have a new boy in our class named Kurtis. Kurtis is so cute! Me and my friend Pam both like him. We both promised each other that we wouldn't tell him. Well guess what happened today? Kurtis left a note in my locker asking me if I liked him.

I want to say yes but Pam might get mad. I like him a lot but so does Pam. Well I'm just going to tell Kurtis yes I like him and maybe we can go out. Pam will get over it, right?

Well gotta go!

Love,

Tabatha

Dear Girls In Real Life Scenarios

Letter #4

Tabatha has made a decision. Write a letter to Tabatha about her decision.

Date _____

Dear Tabatha,

_____

_____

_____

_____

_____

_____

_____

_____

_____

_____

_____

_____

_____

_____

_____

_____

_____

_____

_____

_____

_____

Love,

_____

Dear Diary #5

Meet Armani. The new lip gloss is finally in stores. Armani wrote about it in her diary.

August 17th

Dear Diary,

Today my friends and I went to the mall. Our plan was to get the new Sugar Lips lip gloss but none of us had enough money so we just got the Brown Sugar lip gloss instead.

After we left the store Deena reaches into her pocket and takes out enough Sugar Lips lip gloss for everyone. I know she did not have enough money,

I was the only one who wouldn't take it and Dena said I was trying to be a Miss Goody Two Shoes as always.

The girls were telling me just to take it because it's a gift. When I said no they all started saying things like, I think I'm better than them, I was a stick in the mud and

238

I ruin everything.

I don't think I will hang out with them anymore but if I don't I will be by myself. No friends at all. Decisions, decisions, decisions.

Love,

Armani

Letter #5

Armani is feeling guilty. Write a letter to Armani about how she is feeling.

Date _____

Dear Armani,

_____

_____

_____

_____

_____

_____

_____

_____

_____

_____

_____

_____

_____

_____

_____

_____

_____

_____

Love,

_____

Dear Diary #6

Meet Taylor. She works hard to get straight A's in Science.
Taylor wrote about it in her diary.

June 9th

Dear Diary,

All month Mrs. Brown has been reminding the class about our big science test.

My friend Haley always slacks in science class. Our science test is worth 60% of our final grade and of course she wants to me to let her copy my answers.

She said she hasn't study because she's been too busy. She always says she is too busy to study but if I don't let her copy she will probably get a bad grade plus she is going to be grounded which means she wont be able to come to my party, which means she will miss the surprise. OMG! I don't

know what to do but I am sick of
Haley's excuses. :(

Love,

Taylor

Dear Girls In Real Life Scenarios

Letter #6

Taylor needs some advice about her decision. Write a letter to Taylor to give her some friendly advice.

Date _____

Dear Taylor,

_____

_____

_____

_____

_____

_____

_____

_____

_____

_____

_____

_____

_____

_____

_____

_____

_____

_____

_____

Love,

_____

Dear Diary #7

Meet Faith. Her parents are getting a divorce.   Faith wrote about it in her diary.

September 13th

Dear Diary,

Ugggggghhhh! It's true!!!! My mom and dad are getting a divorce and it's all my fault! I never cleaned my room! My grades are horrible! I never do my chores! And I always make them fight!

Today some dumb counselor lady told us that I was old enough to choose who I want to live with! Why do I have to choose anything? I choose for them to stay together.

OMG! How can I stop this from happening? How could I even let this happen????? I promise I will be on my very best

behavior if they will just work it out. I need a plan to stop this divorce from happening?

 Dear Girls In Real Life Scenarios

And fast! I am so overwhelmed!

Love,

Faith

Simeaka Melton

Letter #7

Faith is overwhelmed with emotion. Write a letter to Faith about how she is feeling.

Date _____

Dear Faith,

_____
_____
_____
_____
_____
_____
_____
_____
_____
_____
_____
_____
_____
_____
_____
_____
_____
_____
_____
_____

Love,

_____

246

Dear Diary #8

Meet Sanaa. There are lots of questions about her eyes. She wrote about it in her diary.

October 13th

Dear Diary,

Here's my problem! My mom has the bright idea that I would like to attend some dumb fashion camp for 2 whole weeks this summer! Ugghh!

Well I guess I would like to go, kinda, BUT I would NOT like to go meet 19 other girls I have never met. All asking me the same old questions. Do you know you have two different color eyes? Why are your eyes two different colors? How did that happen? Do your eyes hurt? Or some will just stare like they have seen a ghost. Oh let's not forget the famous question. Are your eyes like that everyday? Uggggghhhh, some people ask the dumbest questions!

I will never get use to people just staring at me or giving me strange looks.

Ok news flash, I have one brown eye AND one blue eye. Clearly I know that! I wish everybody would stop asking me so many questions about my eyes!!!!

It's embarrassing! I hate all the questions! I just want to be normal! Why am I like this! I wish people would stop staring at me! I wish I could wear sun glasses everyday!

I don't know what to do about fashion camp! On one hand I guess I would really like to go! I love fashion but on the other hand I don't want 19 questions from 19 girls about something I can't help.

That's it, no camp for me. It's just not normal to have 2 different color eyes. Why meeeeee! Why do I have to be the one with weird eyes!!!!

Love,

Sanaa

Letter #8

Sanaa is willing to give up fashion camp. Write a letter to Sanaa about how she is feeling.

Date _____

Dear Sanaa,

_____

_____

_____

_____

_____

_____

_____

_____

_____

_____

_____

_____

_____

_____

_____

_____

_____

_____

_____

_____

Love,

_____

Dear Diary #9

Meet Aaliyah. She has the freckle blues. Aaliyah wrote about it in her diary.

August 9th

Dear Diary,

I hate my freckles! It seems like everyday someone has something to say about them. I've been called freckle face, sprinkle face and even Polka Dot Dotty!

I wish I could do something to cover them up. I have never seen a model with freckles. And I have never seen anyone in those glamour magazines that were proud to have freckles.

Christian told me that he thought my freckles made me special BUT I don't believe that because if everyone is special why am I the only one with freckles?

Anyway I just wanted to say AGAIN
I really hate my freckles!

Love,

Aaliyah

Letter #9

Aaliyah's freckle blues has her feeling down. Write a letter to Aaliyah about how she is feeling.

Date _____

Dear Aaliyah,

_____

_____

_____

_____

_____

_____

_____

_____

_____

_____

_____

_____

_____

_____

_____

_____

_____

_____

_____

Love,

_____

Dear Girls In Real Life Scenarios

Dear Diary #10

Meet Deedra. Her sleepover is coming up and the drama has already started. She wrote about it in her diary.

June 26th

Dear Diary,

My sleepover is in two days and I have a big problem. Kenya and Amanda are my best friends but lately they have not been getting along. My mom said I could only invite one. Even though Amanda starts it most of the time, I don't want them to think I am choosing sides. They are both really excited and I really don't know who to uninvited. Why is there always so much drama!!!!

Love,

Deedra

Letter #10

Deedra has a decision to make and fast. Write a letter to
Deedra about how she is feeling.

Date _____

Dear Deedra,

_____
_____
_____
_____
_____
_____
_____
_____
_____
_____
_____
_____
_____
_____
_____
_____
_____
_____
_____
_____

Love,

_____

Dear Girls In Real Life Scenarios

Journal

255

Simeaka Melton

Date _____

_____

_____

_____

_____

_____

_____

_____

_____

_____

_____

_____

_____

_____

_____

_____

_____

_____

_____

_____

_____

_____

_____

Love,

_____

Dear Girls In Real Life Scenarios

Date _____

_____
_____
_____
_____
_____
_____
_____
_____
_____
_____
_____
_____
_____
_____
_____
_____
_____
_____
_____
_____
_____
_____
_____

Love,

_____

Simeaka Melton

Date _____

_____
_____
_____
_____
_____
_____
_____
_____
_____
_____
_____
_____
_____
_____
_____
_____
_____
_____
_____
_____
_____
_____

Love,

_____

Dear Girls In Real Life Scenarios

Date _____

_____

_____

_____

_____

_____

_____

_____

_____

_____

_____

_____

_____

_____

_____

_____

_____

_____

_____

_____

_____

_____

_____

_____

Love,

_____

Simeaka Melton

Date _____

_____

_____

_____

_____

_____

_____

_____

_____

_____

_____

_____

_____

_____

_____

_____

_____

_____

_____

_____

_____

_____

Love,

_____

Dear Girls In Real Life Scenarios

Date _____

_____
_____
_____
_____
_____
_____
_____
_____
_____
_____
_____
_____
_____
_____
_____
_____
_____
_____
_____
_____
_____
_____

Love,

_____

Simeaka Melton

Date _____

_____
_____
_____
_____
_____
_____
_____
_____
_____
_____
_____
_____
_____
_____
_____
_____
_____
_____
_____
_____
_____
_____
_____

Love,

_____

Dear Girls In Real Life Scenarios

Date _____

_____
_____
_____
_____
_____
_____
_____
_____
_____
_____
_____
_____
_____
_____
_____
_____
_____
_____
_____
_____
_____
_____
_____
_____

Love,

_____

Date _____

_____
_____
_____
_____
_____
_____
_____
_____
_____
_____
_____
_____
_____
_____
_____
_____
_____
_____
_____
_____
_____
_____
_____

Love,

_____

Dear Girls In Real Life Scenarios

Date _____

_____
_____
_____
_____
_____
_____
_____
_____
_____
_____
_____
_____
_____
_____
_____
_____
_____
_____
_____
_____
_____
_____
_____

Love,

_____

Date _____

_____
_____
_____
_____
_____
_____
_____
_____
_____
_____
_____
_____
_____
_____
_____
_____
_____
_____
_____
_____
_____
_____
_____
_____

Love,

_____

Dear Girls In Real Life Scenarios

Date _____

_____
_____
_____
_____
_____
_____
_____
_____
_____
_____
_____
_____
_____
_____
_____
_____
_____
_____
_____
_____
_____
_____

Love,

_____

Simeaka Melton

Date _____

_____
_____
_____
_____
_____
_____
_____
_____
_____
_____
_____
_____
_____
_____
_____
_____
_____
_____
_____
_____
_____
_____
_____

Love,

_____

Dear Girls In Real Life Scenarios

Date _____

_____
_____
_____
_____
_____
_____
_____
_____
_____
_____
_____
_____
_____
_____
_____
_____
_____
_____
_____
_____
_____
_____

Love,

_____

Simeaka Melton

Date _____

_____
_____
_____
_____
_____
_____
_____
_____
_____
_____
_____
_____
_____
_____
_____
_____
_____
_____
_____
_____
_____
_____

Love,

_____

Dear Girls In Real Life Scenarios

Date _____

_____
_____
_____
_____
_____
_____
_____
_____
_____
_____
_____
_____
_____
_____
_____
_____
_____
_____
_____
_____
_____
_____

Love,

_____

Simeaka Melton

Date _____

_____

_____

_____

_____

_____

_____

_____

_____

_____

_____

_____

_____

_____

_____

_____

_____

_____

_____

_____

_____

_____

_____

Love,

_____

Dear Girls In Real Life Scenarios

Date _____

_____

_____

_____

_____

_____

_____

_____

_____

_____

_____

_____

_____

_____

_____

_____

_____

_____

_____

_____

_____

_____

_____

_____

Love,

_____

Simeaka Melton

Date _____

_____
_____
_____
_____
_____
_____
_____
_____
_____
_____
_____
_____
_____
_____
_____
_____
_____
_____
_____
_____
_____
_____
_____

Love,

_____

Dear Girls In Real Life Scenarios

Date _____

_____
_____
_____
_____
_____
_____
_____
_____
_____
_____
_____
_____
_____
_____
_____
_____
_____
_____
_____
_____
_____
_____

Love,

_____

Simeaka Melton

Date _____

_____

_____

_____

_____

_____

_____

_____

_____

_____

_____

_____

_____

_____

_____

_____

_____

_____

_____

_____

_____

_____

Love,

_____

Dear Girls In Real Life Scenarios

Date _____

_____
_____
_____
_____
_____
_____
_____
_____
_____
_____
_____
_____
_____
_____
_____
_____
_____
_____
_____
_____
_____
_____

Love,

_____

Simeaka Melton

Date _____

_____
_____
_____
_____
_____
_____
_____
_____
_____
_____
_____
_____
_____
_____
_____
_____
_____
_____
_____
_____
_____
_____
_____

Love,

_____

Dear Girls In Real Life Scenarios

Date _____

_____
_____
_____
_____
_____
_____
_____
_____
_____
_____
_____
_____
_____
_____
_____
_____
_____
_____
_____
_____
_____
_____
_____

Love,

_____

Simeaka Melton

Date _____

_____
_____
_____
_____
_____
_____
_____
_____
_____
_____
_____
_____
_____
_____
_____
_____
_____
_____
_____
_____
_____
_____
_____
_____

Love,

_____

Dear Girls In Real Life Scenarios

Date _____

_____

_____

_____

_____

_____

_____

_____

_____

_____

_____

_____

_____

_____

_____

_____

_____

_____

_____

_____

_____

_____

_____

_____

Love,

_____

Simeaka Melton

Date _____

_____
_____
_____
_____
_____
_____
_____
_____
_____
_____
_____
_____
_____
_____
_____
_____
_____
_____
_____
_____
_____
_____
_____

Love,

_____

Dear Girls In Real Life Scenarios

Date _____

_____

_____

_____

_____

_____

_____

_____

_____

_____

_____

_____

_____

_____

_____

_____

_____

_____

_____

_____

_____

_____

Love,

_____

Simeaka Melton

Date _____

_____

_____

_____

_____

_____

_____

_____

_____

_____

_____

_____

_____

_____

_____

_____

_____

_____

_____

_____

_____

_____

_____

Love,

_____

Dear Girls In Real Life Scenarios

Date _____

_____

_____

_____

_____

_____

_____

_____

_____

_____

_____

_____

_____

_____

_____

_____

_____

_____

_____

_____

_____

_____

_____

Love,

_____

Activate Your Girl Power!

ABOUT THE AUTHOR

Simeaka Melton is an ordinary girl from Grasonville Maryland living life rising above expectations.

www.Simeaka.com
@Simeaka | @DearGirls | @RAEyouth

61566158R00160

Made in the USA
Lexington, KY
14 March 2017